© 2024 by Michael Gomez

No part of this work may be reproduced without permission except as indicated by the "Fair Use" clause of the copyright law. Passages, images, or ideas taken from this work must be properly credited in any written or published materials.

Table of Contents:

Introductory Aerial of Highway 6……………….1

City of Bryan:

Chapter 1: Texas Avenue……………….................2

Chapter 2: Coulter Drive…………………….…...27

Chapter 3: Texas Avenue, Continued…………...29

Chapter 4: Highway 21………………….............42

Chapter 5: Martin Luther King Jr Street………...48

Chapter 6: Downtown Bryan…………….……...54

Chapter 7: Beck Street…………………….……..72

Chapter 8: William Joel Bryan Parkway………...75

Chapter 9: East 29th Street……………….….......80

Chapter 10: Briarcrest Drive……………….…….92

Chapter 11: Villa Maria Road to FM 2818……...98

Chapter 12: Finfeather Road…………….….…..105

Chapter 13: South College Avenue……….……107

City of College Station:

Chapter 14: University Drive West & Northgate............110

Chapter 15: Wellborn Road……........................126

Chapter 16: George Bush Drive……………..….131

Chapter 17: University Drive East………..…….134

Chapter 18: Earl Rudder Freeway……………....146

Chapter 19: Texas Avenue South……………….149

Chapter 20: Harvey Road ……………….............167

Chapter 21: Holleman Drive………….………...178

Chapter 22: Texas Avenue South, Continued…..180

Chapter 23: Southwest Parkway………………..195

Chapter 24: Texas Avenue South to Highway 6……….198

Closing View of Texas Avenue…………….…...206

Contributions……………………………..…….207

About the Author………………………..……...208

Courtesy of Cushing Memorial Library

Highway 6 and E William Joel Bryan Pkwy, 1980

Chapter 1: Texas Avenue, Bryan

Ramada Inn, 410 S Texas Avenue, College Station

Courtesy of Project HOLD

Courtesy of Cushing Memorial Library

Courtesy of City of Bryan YouTube

Opened in 1963 and in 1980, a 17-floor tower was built next to the main building. During its existence, the hotel has been the Aggieland Inn, University Tower, and The Plaza before it was demolished in 2012. It is now the site of Northpoint Crossing Apartments (opened in 2015), which are high-rise apartments with retail spaces on the first floor.

Tokyo Steak House,
411 Texas Avenue, College Station

Courtesy of Cushing Memorial Library

Opened in 1980 and closed in 1985.

Tokyo Steak House hibachi grill.

Pizza Inn, 413 Texas Avenue, College Station

Shell Station, 425 Texas Avenue, College Station

Courtesy of Cushing Memorial Library

Opened in 1966 and closed in 1986.

Opened in 1968 (exterior seen below) and remodeled in the late 70s. In 1994, the building was remodeled again and became Jim's Food Mart. Jim's Food Mart then became an Exxon Station in the mid 2000s.

Courtesy of Cushing Memorial Library

Luby's Cafeteria, 4401 S Texas Avenue, Bryan

Tom's Barbeque, 4613 Texas Avenue, Bryan

Courtesy of The Eagle

Courtesy of Cushing Memorial Library

Courtesy of YKYFBCS

Opened in 1977 as the area's first Luby's and eventually closed in 2014.

Opened in 1976 and moved to 3601 S College Ave, Bryan in 1985.

Courtesy of 1984 Texas A&M University Yearbook

5

Fajita Rita's, 4501 S Texas Avenue, Bryan

Photo by Dave McDermand from The Eagle

Courtesy of 1991 A&M Consolidated High School Yearbook

Courtesy of A&M Consolidated High School Band Facebook

Originally opened as Chelsea Street Pub in 1979 and became Rebel's Restaurant & Bar in 1980 (seen in far-right picture). Fajita Rita's then opened in 1985 and eventually closed in 2004. The building was a few other restaurants before it was demolished in 2012. It is now the site of First Watch Restaurant, which opened in 2016.

It's Showtime Movie Rentals, 4303 Texas Avenue, Bryan

Courtesy of The Eagle

Opened in 1986 and closed around 1991.

Courtesy of The Eagle

Casa Tomas Restaurant, 4300 Texas Avenue, Bryan

Courtesy of The Eagle

Opened in 1981 as a Southern Mexican Cuisine and eventually closed in 1994.

Courtesy of The Eagle

Half-Price Books, 3828 S Texas Avenue, Bryan

Courtesy of Kovak & Co. Real Estate

Courtesy of The Eagle

Opened in 1982 and moved to 2410 Texas Avenue S in 2000. That location then moved to 1505 University Dr in 2011.

Archie's Taco Bell, 3901 S Texas Avenue, Bryan

Courtesy of 1984 Bryan High School Yearbook

Courtesy of 1984 Bryan High School Yearbook

Opened in 1976 and closed in 1995. It is now the site of Fritella Italian Café.

Video Center, 3517 S Texas Avenue, Bryan

Bobbi's Books & Comics, 3801 Texas Avenue, Bryan

Courtesy of The Eagle

Courtesy of The Eagle

Courtesy of The Eagle

Courtesy of The Eagle

Opened in 1984 and closed in 1998.

Opened in 1986, moving from its original location at 3529 Texas Avenue, Bryan (seen on the left) and closed in 1989.

9

Hong Kong Restaurant,
3805 S Texas Avenue, Bryan

*Photo by Peter Rocha
from The Eagle*

Sign on Texas Avenue

Opened in 1977 and
closed in 1992.

Big State Pawn Shop, 3807 S Texas Avenue, Bryan

Courtesy of The Eagle

Opened in 1986 and became Cash America Pawn in 1991.

Randy Sims Bar-B-Cue, 3824 S Texas Avenue, Bryan

Courtesy of 1983 Bryan High School Yearbook   *Courtesy of 1981 Bryan High School Yearbook*

Opened in 1964 and served what locals claimed to be the
best barbeque in area. After many years, Randy Sims closed
in 1991 and the space became Jose's Restaurant in 1993.

Church's Fried Chicken, 3227 Texas Avenue, Bryan

Kentucky Fried Chicken, 3321 Texas Avenue, Bryan

Opened in 1971 and closed in 2011.

Opened in 1968 and remodeled in the 80s (exterior seen on right) and again in 2008.

Piggly Wiggly, 3516 Texas Avenue, Bryan

Opened in 1970 and closed in 1985.

Courtesy of The Eagle

11

El Chico Restaurant, 3109 S Texas Avenue, Bryan

Courtesy of The Battalion

Opened in 1974 and closed in 1990.

Wendy's, 3216 S Texas Avenue, Bryan

Courtesy of The Eagle

Opened in 1978 and closed in 2008.

Walmart, Manor East Mall, Bryan

Courtesy of The Eagle

Opened in 1982 as the area's first Walmart and was connected to the former Manor East Mall. It eventually closed in 1994 as a new Walmart was built at 2200 Briarcrest Dr, Bryan.

Courtesy of Loopnet.com

Jimmy Jackson Exxon Station, 3000 S Texas Avenue, Bryan

Courtesy of the family of Jimmy Jackson

Opened in 1969 and was demolished in 1998 for an Eckerd Drugs, which became a CVS Pharmacy in 2004.

Courtesy of City of Bryan YouTube

Mr. Gatti's, 2901 S Texas Avenue, Bryan

Courtesy of The Eagle

Opened in 1977 as the second Mr. Gatti's in the area and eventually closed in 1986. In 1988, the space became a Pizza Inn but closed after only a few months. In 1992, China Garden Restaurant opened in the location (seen below) and eventually closed in 2004. In 2005, the building was demolished and is now the site of a Walgreens.

Courtesy of The Eagle

Courtesy of The Eagle
Sign seen on Texas Avenue

Farmer's Market, 2700 Texas Avenue, Bryan

Courtesy of The Eagle

Readfield's Meats & Deli, 2701 Texas Avenue, Bryan

Courtesy of Texashistory.unt.edu

Opened in 1968

Opened in 1971 and closed around 1999.

Courtesy of Texashistory.unt.edu

E-Z Way Drive In, 2612 Texas Avenue, Bryan

Pizza Hut, 2610 Texas Avenue, Bryan

Courtesy of Project HOLD *Courtesy of Kovak & Co. Real Estate*

Opened in 1960 as E-Z Way Drive-In convenience store and became a U Tote M in 1968 (seen in left picture). The store then became E-Z Way again around 1980 and eventually closed in 1990.

Courtesy of 1984 Bryan High School Yearbook

Opened in 1966 as the area's first Pizza Hut and eventually closed in 2002. In 2007, the space became Trevino-Smith Funeral Home.

Allen Oldsmobile-Cadillac, 2401 Texas Avenue, Bryan

Courtesy of Project HOLD

Opened in 1967 and moved to 205 N Earl Rudder Fwy, Bryan in 2002.

McArthur Motel, 2604 Texas Avenue, Bryan

Courtesy of Kovak & Co. Real Estate

Opened in 1957 and closed around 1974. The building was then abandoned for several years until it became Midtown Motel in 1983. Midtown Motel then closed around 1987 and the building was demolished in the early 90s.

Courtesy of Kovak & Co. Real Estate

Holiday Inn Motel, 2300 Texas Avenue, Bryan

Courtesy of Project HOLD

Opened in 1965 and became the Bryan Inn in 1988. Since then, it has been several other motels.

Bryan Post Office, 301 Post Office St

Opened in 1965 and moved in 1990 to 2121 E William Joel Bryan Pkwy as the U.S. Postal Service.

Kroger, 2104 S Texas Avenue, Bryan

Courtesy of The Eagle

Opened in 1977 replacing a former Cooks Store and remodeled in 1991 (seen below). The store eventually closed in 2005 and is now the site of Citi Trends and A&M Furniture.

Courtesy of Csroadsandretail.blogspot.com

Courtesy of The Eagle

Townshire Shopping Center, 1901 S Texas Avenue, Bryan

Opened in 1958 and remodeled in 1982 (seen on right) and again in 2001.

Courtesy of Cushing Memorial Library

Townshire seen in 1983

Courtesy of The Battalion

19

Townshire Shopping Center

Central Texas Hardware "Do-It Center"

Courtesy of Cushing Memorial Library

Opened in 1982, replacing a former Sears store (seen in bottom picture) and closed in 1986. In 1989, Blinn College moved into the space.

Courtesy of Blinn College

Courtesy of The Eagle

Courtesy of 1984 Bryan High School Yearbook

Photo by Bill Meeks from The Eagle

Sears opened in 1958 along with Townshire Shopping Center and closed around 1980.

Townshire Shopping Center

Tri-State Sports Center

Courtesy of The Eagle

Opened in 1983 and moved to 3600 Old College Rd, Bryan in 1988.

Courtesy of The Eagle

Keyser's Crafts & Hobbies

Carboe's Restaurant, 2025 Texas Avenue

Courtesy of The Eagle

Opened in 1983 as a homestyle cooking restaurant and closed in 1986. It is now the site of EZ Pawn.

Baskin Robbin's Ice Cream Plant, 1918 S Texas Avenue, Bryan

U Rent M, 1904 S Texas Avenue, Bryan

Courtesy of Project HOLD

Previously Sanitary Farm Dairies Plant, it became Baskin Robbin's Plant in 1971 and eventually closed in 2001.

Courtesy of Project HOLD

Opened in 1968 as a store to rent power tools, trailers, and tractors. U Rent M eventually closed in 1996 and the building was used for other businesses before being demolished in 2013.

Ken Martin's Steak House, 1803 S Texas Avenue, Bryan

The "Cave Room"

Courtesy of The Battalion

Courtesy of The Battalion

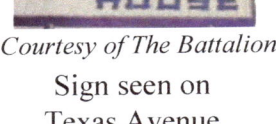
Courtesy of The Battalion
Sign seen on Texas Avenue

Originally The Chicken Shack, the space became Ken Martin's Steak House in 1971. Ken Martin's became a popular restaurant in the area, offering what locals claimed to be the best chicken fried steak along with Youngbloods Restaurant. Ken Martin's also had a soup, salad, and sundae bar. Apart from the main dining room, there was a banquet room called the "cave room", designed as an underground cave with lighting along the walls. After many years, Ken Martin's relocated to 3231 East 29th St, Bryan in 1986.

Courtesy of The Battalion

Monterey House, 1816 S Texas Avenue, Bryan

Courtesy of 1969 Stephen F. Austin High School Yearbook

Opened in 1967 and renamed to Monterey Tex Mex Café around 1991. Monterey Tex Mex Café then closed in 1999 and Taquerias Arandas opened in the location in 2001.

Courtesy of 1971 Stephen F. Austin High School Yearbook

Fat Burger, 1801 Texas Avenue, Bryan

Courtesy of The Eagle

Originally opened as Zuider Zee Seafood Restaurant in 1970 with a signature windmill on the top of the building. Zuider Zee then closed around 1971 and the space became Chick'n Lick'n in 1978 (seen on right) and then Texas Burger shortly after. In 1988, Fat Burger opened in the location and the top part of the building was removed around 2006.

Courtesy of The Eagle

Brazos Business College, 1702 S Texas Avenue, Bryan

Western Sizzlin' Steak House, 1701 S Texas Avenue, Bryan

Courtesy of The Eagle

Courtesy of Cushing Memorial Library

Opened in 1985 and closed in 1993.

Opened in 1976 and closed in 1996.

Courtesy of Carnegie History Center

Courtesy of 1985 Bryan High School Yearbook

25

Lange Music Co., 1410 Texas Avenue, Bryan

Old Woodson Lumber Co., 1106 S Texas Avenue, Bryan

Courtesy of Project HOLD

Opened in 1972 and closed in 1995.

Courtesy of Texashistory.unt.edu

Chapter 2: Coulter Drive, Bryan

Stephen F. Austin Junior High School,
800 S Coulter Dr, Bryan

Courtesy of Texashistory.unt.edu

Originally Stephen F. Austin High School (built in 1939), it served as Bryan's only high school for White and Hispanic students before the integration of Bryan ISD in 1971. It then became a junior high school, serving grades 8-9, and then a middle school (grades 6-8) when Jane Long and Sam Rayburn opened in the early 90s. In 2021, a new campus was built next to the Bryan ISD Performing Arts Center, and now serves grades 7-8.

Tip Top Records and Tapes, 1000 S Coulter Dr, Bryan

Courtesy of Cushing Memorial Library

Opened in 1960 from a converted home (seen on left) and moved across the street to 1005 S Coulter around 1983. Tip Top Records then eventually closed around 1997.

U Tote M, 103 S Coulter Dr, Bryan

Courtesy of The Eagle

Opened in 1962 and became a Circle K in 1984. Prince Food Mart then opened around 1994.

Chapter 3: Texas Avenue, Bryan Continued…

Weingarten's Store

Courtesy of The Eagle

Opened in 1954 and became a Safeway in 1984.

Courtesy of The Battalion

Courtesy of YKYFBCS

Sign seen in the early 80s

Safeway, 1010 S Texas Avenue, Bryan

Courtesy of Google Earth

Opened in 1984 replacing a Weingarten's store and converted into an AppleTree in 1989. AppleTree then closed in 1992 and the space has been used for other businesses throughout the years.

Whataburger, 1101 S Texas Avenue, Bryan

Courtesy of Texashistory.unt.edu

Courtesy of The Battalion

Wyatt's Cafeteria, 804 Texas Avenue, Bryan

Courtesy of Project HOLD

Courtesy of Save the Signs Facebook
Example of the Sign on Texas Avenue

Courtesy of Maps.bryantx.gov

Opened in 1966 and moved to 902 S Texas Avenue in 1988.

Courtesy of 1974 Bryan High School Yearbook

Opened in 1970 and moved to Post Oak Mall in 1985. It is now the site of the MHMR Authority of Brazos Valley.

31

Klechka Piano & Organ Co, 405 Texas Avenue, Bryan

Courtesy of Google Earth

Opened around 1976 and offered a large selection of pianos, organs, and keyboards for many years. Klechka Piano eventually closed in the early 2010s and the building demolished around 2015.

Wienerschnitzel, 501 Texas Avenue, Bryan

Courtesy of Carnegie History Center

Courtesy of Texashistory.unt.edu
Sign on Texas Avenue

Opened in 1969

Courtesy of Carnegie History Center

Bryan Tire & Wheel, 400 S Texas Avenue, Bryan

Sinclair Gas Station, 507 S Texas Avenue, Bryan

Courtesy of Texashistory.unt.edu

Courtesy of Texashistory.unt.edu

Bryan City Hall, 300 Texas Avenue, Bryan

Courtesy of 150.bryantx.gov

Courtesy of Insite Magazine

Opened in 1987

Bryan Police Department, 111 East 27th St, Bryan

Courtesy of Carnegie History Center

Courtesy of City of Bryan Flickr

Moved to 301 S Texas Avenue in 1986
and then to 303 East 29th St in 2008.

Texas Avenue and William Joel Bryan Pkwy, Bryan

Courtesy of Carnegie History Center

Zip'N Gas Station, 200 N Texas Avenue, Bryan

Courtesy of The Eagle

Courtesy of Google Earth

Originally Nash's Self-Service Station (seen on left), it became a Zip'N in 1987. The Zip'N was then torn down along with an auto repair shop (seen below) for a strip mall in 2011. The strip mall now houses a larger Zip'N along with other tenants.

Just Brakes, 208 N Texas Avenue, Bryan

Opened in the early 80s and closed in 1988. The space was used for other auto repair shops throughout the years until the building was demolished in 2011.

Courtesy of Just Brakes Facebook

35

Safeway, 201 N Texas Avenue, Bryan

Courtesy of Cushing Memorial Library  *Courtesy of Maps.bryantx.gov*  *Photo by Bill Meeks from The Eagle*

Opened in 1950 with the entrance originally facing away from Texas Avenue. In 1969, a full remodel was done, and the new store faced Texas Avenue. The store eventually closed in 1986, and the building has since been used for the Brazos County Health Department.

Burger Boy, 300 N Texas Avenue, Bryan

Opened in 1964 as Dairy Burger and became Burger Boy in 1978. Burger Boy then closed in 1989 and the space became Backyard BBQ in 1990. La Familia Restaurant then opened in 1991 and the drive in was demolished in the 90s for an indoor building.

Courtesy of 1967 Stephen F. Austin High School Yearbook

Archie's 39¢ Hamburger Place, 310 N Texas Avenue, Bryan

Photo by Dave McDermand from The Eagle

Courtesy of The Eagle

Courtesy of Carnegie History Center

Opened in 1985 and became Hot Dogs Etc. in 1990.

Seen from an Aerial View

The Butcher Block, 600 N Texas Avenue, Bryan

Courtesy of 1982 Bryan High School Yearbook

Opened in 1982 and closed in 1988.

Texas Inn, 506 N Texas Avenue, Bryan

Church's Fried Chicken, 507 N Texas Avenue, Bryan

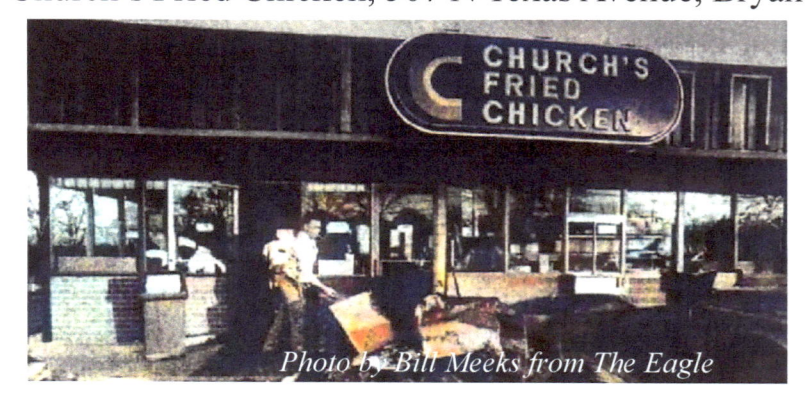

Courtesy of Texashistory.unt.edu

Photo by Bill Meeks from The Eagle

Opened in 1965 as Van's Motel and became the Texas Inn in 1981. The building was then demolished in the early 2000s and is now the site of Q Beauty store.

Opened in 1972

Popeye's, 720 N Texas Avenue, Bryan

Courtesy of Google Earth

Opened in 1985 and became John's Katfish Kitchen in 1988 and then Gath's Chicken in 1989. The space has since been used for several restaurants.

Tinsley's Chicken, 705 N Texas Avenue, Bryan

Courtesy of The Eagle

Opened in 1973 and renamed to Ron's Fried Chicken in 1988. Since then, the space has been used for several other restaurants.

39

Billups Gas Station, 720 N Texas Avenue, Bryan

Courtesy of The Eagle

Opened in 1978 and became a Charter Food Store around 1986 and then a Circle K in 1991. Circle K then became an Everyday Store around 2000 and then Town & Country Food Mart in 2002, which is still open today.

Kon Tiki Lounge, 1225 N Texas Avenue, Bryan

Opened in the late 60s and became a popular nightclub in the black community. The club moved to a new building in 1971 (seen above) and eventually closed in 1992. Since then, the space was used for other clubs throughout the years until the building was demolished in 2012.

1223 N Texas Avenue, Bryan

Courtesy of Google Earth

Became Tom's Lounge around 1984 and then Disco Down Club in 1988. The space then became Dee's Club in 1994 (seen above) and stayed open for many years until it's closure in 2011. The building was then demolished in 2012.

J.J.'s Liquor, 1219 N Texas Avenue, Bryan

Courtesy of Google Earth

Opened in 1978 and closed around 2011.

Texas Department of Transportation, 1300 N Texas Avenue, Bryan

Courtesy of Texashistory.unt.edu

Originally the Texas Highway Department, it became the Texas Department of Transportation in the early 70s. In 2012, the department then moved to a new facility at 2591 N Earl Rudder Fwy, Bryan.

Weiner's, 1520 N Texas Avenue, Bryan

Courtesy of Project HOLD

Opened in 1972 and became a popular clothing store that provided the latest fashions at affordable prices. After many years, Weiner's closed in 2001 and the space became Best Pawn. Best Pawn eventually closed in 2021 and the building was remodeled for Poco Loco Supermercado in 2023.

Chapter 4: Highway 21, Bryan

City Heat Bar & Grill, 1000 San Jacinto Ln, Bryan

Courtesy of The Eagle *Courtesy of The Eagle*

Originally The Royal Club, which was a popular nightclub in the black community dating back to the 1960s. The Royal Club closed in the early 80s and the space became City Heat Bar & Grill around 1986 and then Hard Times Bar in 1989. In 1995, the space became San Jacinto Restaurant and then Minnie Faces Soul Food Restaurant in 2000. The building was then remodeled in the mid 2000s and has been used for other businesses throughout the years.

Shannon's Café, 601 San Jacinto Ln, Bryan

Opened in 1970 and moved into a new building around 2016.

Courtesy of Up From Cotton

Lone Star Grocery, 710 San Jacinto Ln, Bryan

Opened around 1964 and closed in the late 2010s.

Courtesy of Google Earth

Highway 21, Bryan

Courtesy of The Courier

Courtesy of Google Earth

Courtesy of Brazos Valley Area-Wide Phone Book

Courtesy of Insite Magazine

Courtesy of The Eagle

The Red Bandana Buffet

Courtesy of Carnegie History Center

Safeway, 2001 E State Hwy 21, Bryan

Courtesy of The Eagle

Courtesy of The Eagle

Opened in 1986 and became an AppleTree in 1989. Appletree then closed in 2009 and the space became El Ahorro Supermarket in 2010 and then La Michoacana Meat Market in 2013.

Longhorn Tavern Steak House, 1609 N Texas Avenue, Bryan

Courtesy of Longhorn Tavern Steakhouse Facebook

Courtesy of YKYFBCS

Opened around 1978 and moved to 201 East 24th St, Bryan in 2009. The building was then demolished in 2011 for an H-E-B.

Relax Inn, 3604 E State Hwy 21, Bryan

Courtesy of The Eagle

Opened in 1983

McDonald's, 2930 E State Hwy 21, Bryan

Courtesy of Brazos Heritage Society

Opened in 1985 and originally had an outdoor Playplace with a patio cover. In 2005, the building was remodeled and the Playplace was removed, giving it a more modern look.

Red Patio Cover   Outdoor Playplace

46

Bernath Concrete, 2400 Hwy 21 E, Bryan

Courtesy of Project HOLD

Opened around 1958 and closed around 1993.

Nuche's Convenience Store, 2907 Hwy 21 E, Bryan

Courtesy of The Eagle

Opened in 1969 and became Bryan Food Xchange in the late 90s.

Chapter 5: Martin Luther King Jr Street, Bryan

George Washington Carver School, 1401 W Martin Luther King Jr St, Bryan

Courtesy of Texashistory.unt.edu *Courtesy of Texashistory.unt.edu*

Opened in 1949 as an elementary school for black students (grades 1-7) who lived on the West Side of Bryan. Previously, students had to walk to Washington Elementary School, located on the East Side at 500 East 20th St. After Bryan ISD integrated in 1971, Carver and E.A. Kemp High School became schools for 6th grade students for many years. In 1992, Carver renovated and became Carver Early Childhood Center. The front building (seen above) was demolished leaving the two rear buildings of the school. In 2011, Carver and Kemp Elementary School merged into Kemp-Carver Elementary, located at 750 Bruin Trce.

Aerial view of the five blocks that are now Neal Elementary & Neal Park

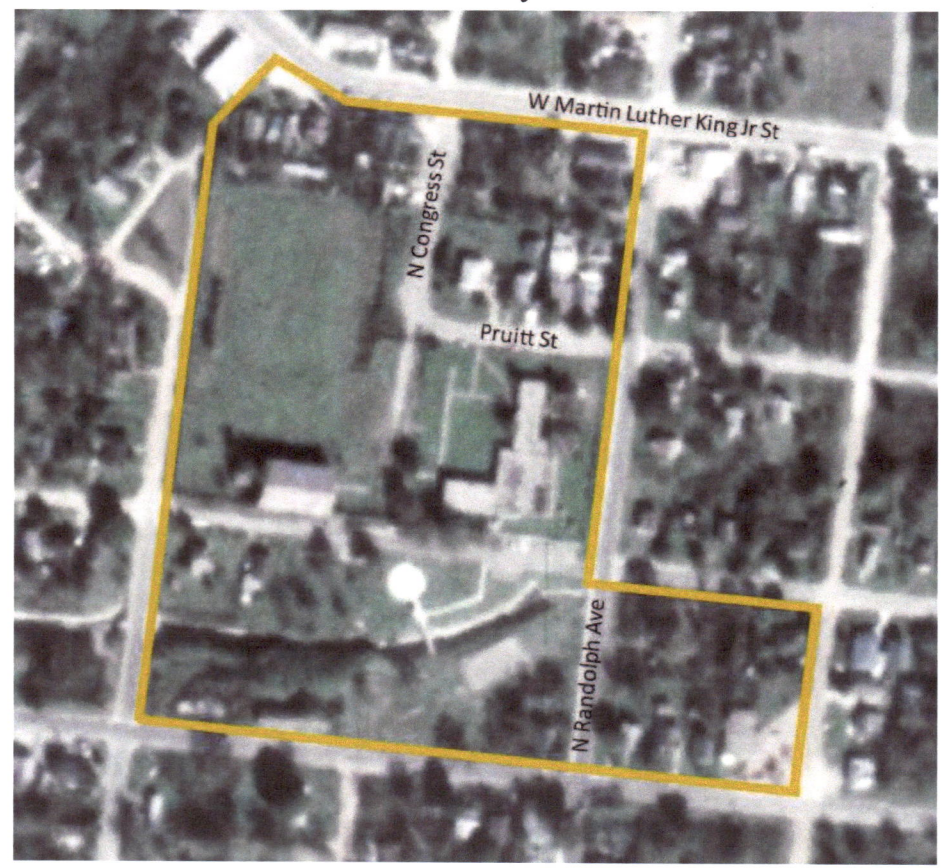

Courtesy of Historicaerials.com

Neal Campus, 600 N Congress St, Bryan

Courtesy of 1958 Kemp High School Yearbook

Originally Kemp High School, it became Neal Junior High when E.A. Kemp High School (located on W Martin Luther King Jr St) opened in 1961. When Bryan ISD integrated in 1971, the campus became an alternative school and daycare for many years. In 1996, five entire blocks were razed to build Neal Elementary School and Neal Recreation Center, which opened in 1998. This project also renovated Williams Park and renamed it to Neal Park. As stated from a 1976 survey: Williams Park was 2 acres and had playgrounds, a basketball court, picnic tables, and ponds. The construction of the new school and park removed a portion of N Congress St, N Randolph Ave, and 20th St (now Pruitt St).

Courtesy of 1958 Kemp High School Yearbook

The Place, 702 W 20th St, Bryan

Originally Scott's Diner, it became The Place in the early 70s, which was a popular nightclub among black residents. The exterior looked like a white house and was owned by the late Garfield Scott. It was known to be a more formal club, as payment was collected at the door and a dress code was enforced. Within the club was a dance floor with mirrors along the walls, a seating area, and bar. The Place eventually closed around 1992 and the building was demolished for Neal Elementary School in 1996.

Courtesy of Maps.bryantx.gov

THE PLACE
702 W. 20th Bryan

Courtesy of The Eagle

Mosley's Grocery & Laundromat, 701 W Martin Luther King Jr St, Bryan

Courtesy of Up from Cotton

Owned by the late Sam Mosley, the store opened in 1936 and became a staple in the black community, selling meats, produce, and other goods. The store also had a laundromat inside and a gas pump in its early days. Mosley's eventually closed in the late 70s and the building was demolished for Neal Elementary School in 1996.

Courtesy of The Eagle
Bryan City Council visits The Harlem

Courtesy of Maps.bryantx.gov

The Harlem Club, 600 W 22nd St, Bryan

Owned by the late Deoliver Crenshaw, she opened The Harlem in the late 60s and it became a popular nightclub in the black community. After many years, the club closed in 1996 and the building was demolished the same year for Neal Park.

Dairy Queen, 216 W Martin Luther King Jr St, Bryan

Courtesy of The Eagle

Opened in 1974 and closed around 1982.

Cash Food Market, 200 W Martin Luther King Jr St, Bryan

Opened around 1973 and closed in the late 2000s.

Courtesy of Texashistory.unt.edu

Ice House on Main, 800 N Main St, Bryan

Courtesy of The Eagle

Became Cell Block 5 club in 1979 (sign can be seen above), which offered a mix of country, disco, and rock music. The club closed shortly after in 1981, and the space has been used for other venues throughout the years.

Early 20th Century homes on E Martin Luther King Jr St

Courtesy of Texashistory.unt.edu

Courtesy of Texashistory.unt.edu

Sarge's Club, 617 E Martin Luther King Jr St, Bryan

SARGE'S CLUB | Opened around 1988 and renamed to Twice as Nice in 1992 and then Club Be Nice in 1995. Since then, the space has been for several other venues.
617 E. MLK

Courtesy of The Eagle

Ben's Grocery, 1101 E Martin Luther King Jr St, Bryan

Opened in 1971 and closed around 1998.

Courtesy of The Eagle

Chapter 6: Downtown Bryan

North Main St, Bryan, 1986

Courtesy of Texashistory.unt.edu

55

Curtis Mathes Televisions, 201 N Main St, Bryan

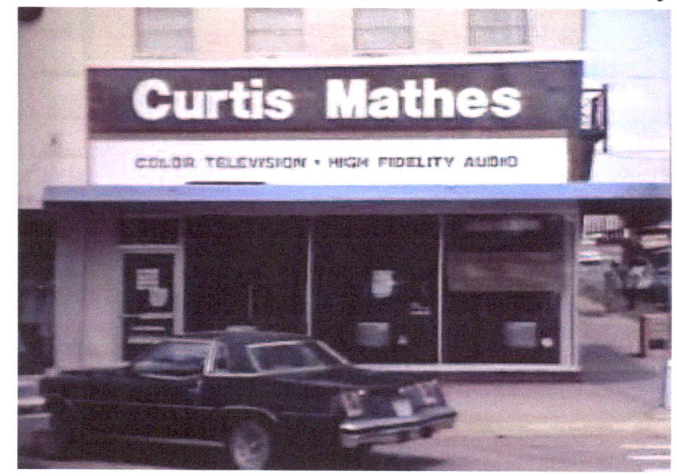

Courtesy of Archive.org

Opened in 1978 and moved to 1123 E Villa Maria Rd, Bryan in 1984.

Colortyme TV Rental, 201 N Main St, Bryan

Courtesy of Texashistory.unt.edu

Opened in 1980 and moved to 1300 Texas Avenue, Bryan in 1990.

Woolworth's, 110 N Main St, Bryan

Courtesy of Texashistory.unt.edu

Opened in 1973 and closed in 1991.

K. Wolens, 221 N Main St, Bryan

Courtesy of Carnegie History Center

Opened in 1951 and closed in 1985.

Courtesy of Project HOLD

57

Brown's Shoe Fit, 113 N Main St — Heritage Menswear, 117 N Main St — Catalena Hatters, 203 N Main St

Opened in 1972 and moved to the Redmond Terrace Center, College Station in 1982.

Opened in 1974 and closed in 2014.

Opened in 1983

Twin City Furniture, 219 N Main St, Bryan

Courtesy of Texashistory.unt.edu

Opened in 1982 and closed around 1995.

Court's Saddlery, 403 N Main St, Bryan

Courtesy of Texashistory.unt.edu

Opened in 1969 and closed in the mid 2000s. The building was then demolished around 2011 and is now the site of Park Station Apartments.

Piggly Wiggly, 200 East 24th St, Bryan

Courtesy of Carnegie History Center

Opened in 1970 from a previous Orr's Supermarket and closed in 1985.

Palace Theatre, 105 S Main St, Bryan, 1986

Courtesy of Texashistory.unt.edu

Opened in 1929 and went through a few remodels over the decades with it's last being in 1968 (exterior seen above). The theatre closed in 1986 after the roof collapsed and the building was sold to the City of Bryan. The building was then demolished and rebuilt in 1995 as an amphitheater.

Carnegie Public Library, 111 S Main St, Bryan, 1986

Courtesy of Texashistory.unt.edu

South Main St, Bryan, 1986

Courtesy of Texashistory.unt.edu

South Main St, Bryan, 1985

Courtesy of Emporis.com

Bryan Hospital, 117 S Regent Avenue, Bryan

Courtesy of Google Earth

Opened in 1943 and remodeled in 1955 (exterior seen above). The hospital eventually closed in the late 2000s and in 2011, the building and a portion of N Washington Avenue were demolished for Roy Kelley Parking Garage.

Courtesy of Carnegie History Center

Courtesy of Google Earth
View of N Washington Avenue

Blinn College, 200 N Main St, Bryan

Courtesy of Carnegie History Center

Opened in 1972 and moved to the Townshire Shopping Center in 1989.

Central Texas Hardware, 202 S Bryan Avenue, Bryan

Courtesy of Texashistory.unt.edu

Dating back to 1919, Central Texas Hardware was a prominent business for tools, parts, and other home improvement needs. The store eventually closed in 1986 and the space has been used for several businesses throughout the years.

The Attic Antiques, 118 S Bryan Avenue, Bryan

Courtesy of Carnegie History Center

Opened in 1974

Milton Franklin Furniture, 201 W 26th St, Bryan

Courtesy of Texashistory.unt.edu

Opened in 1951 and offered appliances, furniture, antiques, and electronics. After many years, the store closed in 1990 and is now the site of Mr. G's Italian Pizzeria (opened in 1996).

Old Bryan Post Office, 216 W 26th St, Bryan

Courtesy of Texashistory.unt.edu

Vick Pharmacy, 200 W 26th St, Bryan, 1982

Courtesy of 150.bryantx.gov

Courtesy of Texashistory.unt.edu

Became Medical Center Pharmacy in 1984 and closed around 2007. It is now the site of Rx Pizza.

Old Universal Service Station, 307 W 26th St, Bryan

Courtesy of Texashistory.unt.edu

Bowie Elementary School, 401 W 26th St, Bryan

Courtesy of Texashistory.unt.edu

Dating back to 1918, Bowie School was open for many decades until it's closure in 1991. The building was left vacant for many years until it was renovated in 2019. It is now office space for Gessner Engineering, Vaughn Construction, and has a barber shop named Bowie Barbers.

Los Norteños Cafe, 201 N Main St, Bryan

Los Norteños has moved, but the old sign still hangs over the new Dos Hermanos restaurant.

Opened in 1985 and moved next door to 205 S Main St in 1987. The restaurant eventually closed in 2012 and is now the site of Sparrow Lane Home Goods.

Zarape Restaurant, 308 N Main St, Bryan

Photo by Bill Meeks from The Eagle   *Courtesy of Jose's Restaurant*

Opened in 1980 and closed in 2008.

69

Food Town, 600 N Main St, Bryan

Courtesy of Carnegie History Center

Food Town was a grocery store known for its affordable groceries and restaurant that served homestyle food. Originally located at 516 N Main St, it moved to this location in 1973 and provided more parking for customers. Food Town eventually closed in 2000 and the building was demolished around 2009.

Old Kimbell Feed Co., 607 N Main St, Bryan

Courtesy of Texashistory.unt.edu

First Baptist Church, 200 S Texas Avenue, Bryan

Courtesy of Texashistory.unt.edu

Courtesy of Texashistory.unt.edu

With a history dating back to the 19th Century, the Sanctuary building was constructed in 1928 (seen on left) and a new educational building was added in the 1970s (seen on right). The Sanctuary was demolished in the early 90s and the church operated in the educational building until 2007. The space then became the Brazos County Administration Building in 2008.

Chapter 7: Beck Street, Bryan

Christopher Village Apartments, 1200 Ridgedale St, Bryan

Courtesy of Historicaerials.com

Courtesy of The Battalion

Courtesy of The Eagle

Christopher Village was built in 1971 as housing for low-income residents and renamed to Mockingbird Run Apartments in 1987. After many years, the apartments were demolished in 1999, and the land is now an extension of Henderson Park, which was originally a small park located at 1500 Ridgedale St.

Burger Inn, 1400 Beck St, Bryan

Courtesy of 1978 Bryan High School Yearbook

Opened in 1976 and closed around 1983.

U Tote M, 1305 Beck St, Bryan

City of Bryan razes Circle K
Courtesy of The Eagle

Street crews tear down an abandoned Circle K at 1305 Beck in Bryan that previously had been condemned by the city. The demolition was part of an ongoing effort by the city to stifle gang- and drug-related activities.
Photo by Mike C. Mulvey

Opened in 1964 and became a Circle K in 1984. Circle K then closed in 1989 and the building was demolished shortly after in 1990 due to gang and drug related activities.

Aerial View of the Store

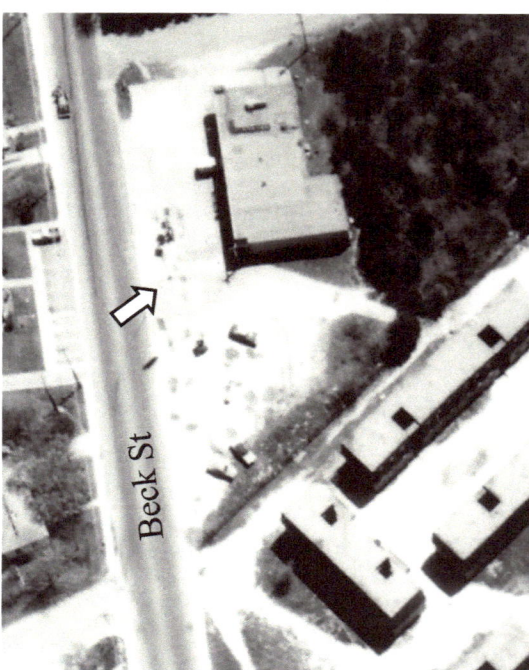

Beck St

Courtesy of Maps.bryantx.gov

74

Chapter 8: William Joel Bryan Parkway, Bryan

U Tote M, 1208 W Wm J Bryan Pkwy, Bryan

Courtesy of Google Earth

Opened around 1965 and became a Circle K in 1984. Circle K then closed in 1989.

Dixie Tire Co., 301 W Wm J Bryan Pkwy, Bryan

Courtesy of Texashistory.unt.edu

Opened in 1985

Boys & Girls Club of the Brazos Valley, 900 W Wm J Bryan Pkwy, Bryan

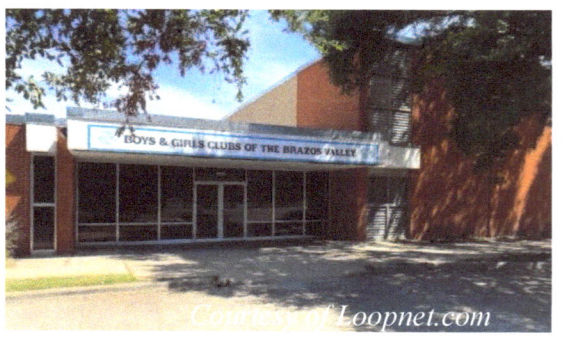

Courtesy of Google Earth

Courtesy of Loopnet.com

Opened in 1964 as the Boys Club and became the Boys & Girls club in 1990. The club eventually moved to a new facility at 1910 Beck St, Bryan in 2022.

Perry's, 208 N Bryan Avenue, Bryan

Courtesy of Project HOLD

Opened in 1964 as a five and dime store, selling household goods, clothing, and shoes. Perry's eventually closed around 1981 and the space was left vacant for many years until the building was remodeled in 2001.

Courtesy of Carnegie History Center

Old First National Bank, 100 W William J Bryan Pkwy, Bryan

Courtesy of Texashistory.unt.edu

Western Auto, 300 E Wm J Bryan Pkwy, Bryan

Courtesy of 1970 Stephen F. Austin High School Yearbook

Opened in 1953 as an auto parts and accessories store. The store closed in 1980 and became the Brazos County Election Administration.

Beetle's BBQ, 201 E Wm J Bryan Pkwy, Bryan

Courtesy of YKYFBCS

Opened in 1989 and closed in 1998.

Dairy Queen & Tenneco Gas Station, E William Joel Bryan Pkwy, Bryan

Tanner's Dairy Queen opened in 1987 and closed in 2003 after many years. It is now the site of La Botana Mexican Restaurant.

Courtesy of Kovak & Co. Real Estate

Courtesy of The Courier

The Tenneco Station is now a Valero Station.

79

Chapter 9: East 29th Street, Bryan

North Texas Avenue, Bryan, early 80s

Texas Avenue and East 29th St, Bryan, early 80s

Courtesy of Carnegie History Center

Fina Station, 300 Texas Avenue, Bryan

Was demolished for Bryan City Hall in 1987.

Courtesy of Carnegie History Center

Courtesy of Cushing Memorial Library

81

Greyhound Station, 405 East 29th St, Bryan

https://www.flickr.com/photos/katherineofchicago/3137762602

Originally a U Tote M store, it became a Greyhound Station in 1976 and moved to 1134 Finfeather Rd, Bryan in 2005.

Photo by David Einsel from The Eagle

AM/PM Clinic, 401 S Texas Avenue, Bryan

Courtesy of Google Earth

Originally Twin City International Dealership, the space became AM/PM Clinic in 1983. AM/PM Clinic then became North Clinic around 1991 and then Texas Avenue Medical Clinic around 1997. Texas Avenue Medical Clinic then closed in 2007 and the building was demolished the same year for a Burger King. Burger King then became a Chicken Express in 2012 and is still open today.

7-Eleven, 900 East 29th St, Bryan

Courtesy of The Eagle

Opened around 1980 and closed in 1991. The building was demolished the same year and has since been a vacant lot.

Fannin Elementary School, 1200 Baker Avenue, Bryan

Originally Bryan High School and then Lamar Junior High, it became Fannin Elementary School in 1957. After many years, the old building was demolished for a new campus in 1989, which incorporated parts of the old building such as the front pillars.

Courtesy of Texashistory.unt.edu

Courtesy of Texashistory.unt.edu

Schulman 6 Theater, 2002 East 29th St, Bryan

Courtesy of Cushing Memorial Library

College Park 6

Courtesy of The Battalion

The Schulman 6 was a six-screen theater located in front of the former Skyway Twin Drive-In. It was owned by the Schulman family, who owned several theaters in town such as the Palace Theater and Manor East III. The Schulman 6 opened in 1982 and became popular among residents as it offered $1 movie nights. After many years, the theater was renamed to the College Park 6 when Blinn College was built in 1997. The College Park 6 eventually closed in 2002 and became the Blinn College Bookstore.

U Tote M, 2613 East 29th St, Bryan

Courtesy of Project HOLD

Opened around 1973 and became a Circle K in 1984. Circle K then closed in 1989.

St. Joseph Hospital, 2801 Franciscan Dr, Bryan

Courtesy of Carnegie History Center

Seen in 1987

Ken Martin's Steak House, 3231 East 29th St, Bryan

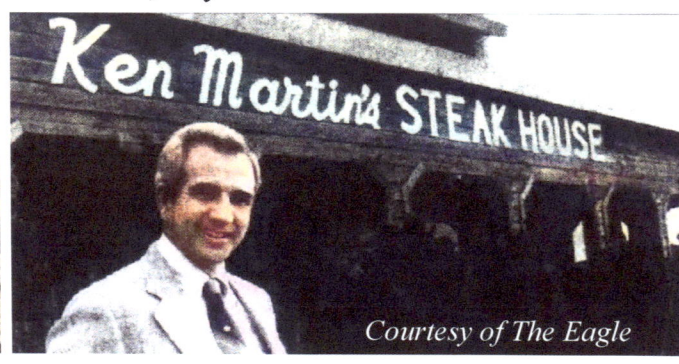

Courtesy of Brazos Valley Area-Wide Phone Book

Courtesy of The Eagle

Owner Ken Martin can be seen

Opened in 1982 as Pacific Coast Highway Restaurant and became
Ken Martin's Steak House in 1986. In 2006, the restaurant was
renamed to Ken Martin's Safari Grille and eventually closed in 2011.

Salad Bar

Dining Area

Photos Courtesy of Brazos Valley Area-Wide Phone Book

Briarcrest Drive and East 29th St, Bryan

Courtesy of Carnegie History Center

Little Caesars in the Briarcrest Center

Courtesy of The Eagle

7-Eleven, 3330 East 29th St, Bryan

Courtesy of 1984 Bryan High School Yearbook

Located on the corner of the intersection was originally a strip mall housing a 7-Eleven and Lube King that opened in 1979. In 1986, a Little Caesars opened in the Briarcrest Center across the street and moved next to the 7-Eleven in 1991. In 2001, the strip mall was demolished for a Walgreens, which is still open today.

7-Eleven sign can be seen

Photo by Bill Meeks from The Eagle

Arby's, 3501 East 29th St, Bryan

Courtesy of Carnegie History Center

Opened in 1983 and became a Taco Bell in 1996.

Courtesy of Loopnet.com
Example of the building

Excalibre Club, 1803 Greenfield Plaza, Bryan

Courtesy of The Eagle

Courtesy of The Eagle

Courtesy of The Eagle

Opened in 1982, replacing a former Pizza Inn. The club then closed in 1989 and is now the site of the Bryan Community Development office.

U Tote M, 3900 East 29th St, Bryan

Courtesy of Project HOLD

Opened around 1969 and became a Circle K in 1984. Circle K then closed in 1987.

East 29th St. Warehouse, 3715 East 29th St, Bryan

Courtesy of Project HOLD

Opened in 1973 and closed in 1987.

Glassware • Stuffed Animals • Posters & Prints
Baskets • Silk & Dried Flowers • Imported Soaps & Toiletries • Stationery • Frames • Kitchenware • Precious Moment Gifts • Sterling Silver Jewelry • Paper & Party Goods • Potpourri & Simmering Scents

East 29th St. Warehouse

846-2408   Town & Country Shopping Center   VISA/MC

Courtesy of The Battalion

Carter Creek Shopping Center, 4001 East 29th St, Bryan

Winn-Dixie Marketplace

Courtesy of Former Texas Division Associates Facebook

Opened in 1985 and closed in 2002. In 2004, The Brazos Valley Council of Governments moved into the space and is still open today.

Tubby's Barbeque

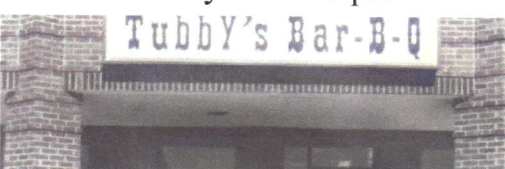

Courtesy of 1989 Bryan High School Yearbook

DoubleDave's Pizzaworks

Opened in 1987 and moved to 2002 East 29th St in 1998.

1985 Directory

CHRISTY'S FLOWERS
Isn't it time your house was blooming? The smell of Spring is waiting for you at Christy's, where every arrangement is a work of art.

DOUBLE DAVES
Hungry for pizza? No problem. Double Daves is doubly delicious and waiting for you. Give us a call or come by for the premiere pizza in the Bryan/College Station area.

DOY'S HALLMARK SHOP
Nothing says it better than a card from Hallmark. If you're looking for something special, shop Doy's and discover cards, stuffed animals, unique gifts and more. Show you care with a gift from Hallmark.

FANTASTIC SAMS
Fantastic Sams has everything to keep you looking your best. Fantastic cuts at a fantastic price, that's Fantastic Sam's.

MARY LYNN'S DRESS SHOP
They'll know your somebody when you step out in style in an outfit from Mary Lynn's. Warm up your wardrobe with the newest arrivals at Mary Lynn's, where shopping is fun.

OLAN MILLS
Capture that smile in a portrait by Olan Mills. Graduation, birthday, wedding or anniversary, anytime is the right time for Olan Mills. Call today for an appointment and give the gift that will be treasured forever.

STYLISH PRIVY
Dress up your bathroom with beautiful soaps, monogrammed towels and super soft bathmats. Stylish Privy has everything you need to add that personal touch of style to any privy.

SUNTAN SALON
Why let your tan fade away? Keep that radiant glow all year long with a suntan from the Suntan Salon. All others pale in comparison.

WINN DIXIE
So much more than a grocery store, Winn Dixie has everything to help you with your household needs. Let our delicious bakery and deli help with your everyday cooking. Fresh meats and quality produce keep our customer's coming back. Shop Winn Dixie, the cornerstone of Carter Creek, for the low prices and friendly service you deserve.

BILL'S BAR-B-Q
Great traditional smoked bar-b-que in a comfortable family atmosphere. The smoky aroma is so good that it's hard to pass by without stopping, at almost any time of day.

Courtesy of The Eagle

Courtesy of The Eagle

National Video Superstore, Carter Creek Center, Bryan

Opened in 1987 and became Box Office Video in 1990. Box Office Video then closed in the late 90s.

Courtesy of The Battalion

East 29th St, Bryan, 1983

Photo by David Einsel from The Eagle

Chapter 10: Briarcrest Drive, Bryan

First City Bank, 3000 Briarcrest Dr, Bryan

Courtesy of The Eagle

Opened in 1985 and became Victoria Bank & Trust in 1993 and then Northwest Banks around 1997 (seen on left). It is now the site of Wells Fargo Bank.

Courtesy of The Eagle

Fred Brown Mazda, 3100 Briarcrest Dr, Bryan

Courtesy of The Eagle

Opened in 1984 and changed hands to Gary Shelton Mazda in 2001. It is now the site of Douglass Mazda.

93

Safeway, 1805 Briarcrest Dr, Bryan

Courtesy of Google Earth

Old Safeway sign, which was since been taken down.

Courtesy of Google Earth

Courtesy of Cushing Memorial Library

Opened in 1977 as the largest Safeway in Bryan and moved across the street to 1760 Briarcrest Dr in 1988. Around 1991, Brazos Bingo opened in the location, and is still open today. As of now, the space has two tenants, with the other half being Antioch Community Church, which opened in the early 2010s.

Safeway, 1760 Briarcrest Dr, Bryan

https://www.flickr.com/photos/16441604@N07/2620202438

Courtesy of The Eagle

Courtesy of The Eagle

Opened in 1988 (moving from 1805 Briarcrest Dr) and became an AppleTree in 1989. AppleTree then closed in 2008 and the space became Village Foods Store. In 2016, Village Foods closed, and an Aldi opened in the location.

Galleria Village, 1716 Briarcrest Dr, Bryan

Courtesy of Insite Magazine

Opened in 1989

Steak & Ale Restaurant, 1710 Briarcrest Dr, Bryan

Courtesy of The Texas Aggie Magazine

Opened in 1984 and became Oxford Street Restaurant in 1988. Oxford Street then closed in 2008 and the building was eventually demolished in 2012.

Inside Oxford Street Restaurant

Courtesy of The Eagle *Courtesy of The Eagle*
Salad Bar Full-service Bar

Ardan Catalog Showroom, 1673 Briarcrest Dr, Bryan

Courtesy of Insite Magazine

Opened in 1979 and closed in 1986.

Courtesy of The Eagle

Became Rolling Thunder Skating Rink in 1989 and then Mr. Gatti's in 1996. Mr. Gatti's then moved to 2026 Texas Avenue S, College Station in 2003. The space was then Thunder Elite recreation center from 2007 to 2011 and is now Planet Fitness (opened in 2014).

Chapter 11: Villa Maria Road, Bryan

McDonald's, 825 W Villa Maria Rd, Bryan

Brazos Blue Ribbon Bakery, 1136 E Villa Maria Rd, Bryan

Courtesy of The Eagle   *Courtesy of Insite Magazine*

Opened in 1985 as Bill Ford Auto Supply and closed in 1986. The space then became Brazos Blue Ribbon Bakery in 1989 and then Must Be Heaven in 1999. In 2021, Must Be Heaven renamed to Sweet Relish Café.

Courtesy of 1992 Bryan High School Yearbook

Opened in 1979 and remodeled in 2000, and again in 2018 with a more modern look.

Manor East Mall, 1127 E Villa Maria Rd, Bryan

Courtesy of City of Bryan YouTube

Originally a shopping center, it opened as an indoor mall in 1970. After many years, Manor East Mall eventually closed in 2004 due to competition from Post Oak Mall. The Tejas Center was built the same year, and a portion of the mall was demolished for an H-E-B with the rest being remodeled for other stores.

Hastings, 725 E Villa Maria Rd, Bryan

Courtesy of YKYFBCS

Opened in 1989 and remodeled in 2006. Hastings then closed in 2017 as the last location in the area, and the space became a Marshalls in 2018.

Taco Villa, 614 E Villa Maria Rd, Bryan

Courtesy of The Battalion

Opened in 1979 and became a Del Taco in 1985. In 1990, Quick as a Flash opened in the location and then became a Ritz Camera in 1998. The space then became a RadioShack in 2006 and eventually closed in 2015. It is now the site of Fred Loya Insurance.

Tinsley's Chicken 'N Rolls, 612 E Villa Maria Rd, Bryan

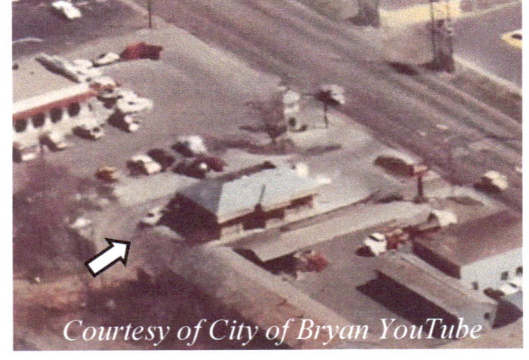

Courtesy of City of Bryan YouTube

Courtesy of Archive.org
Example of the building

Opened in 1979 and became Ron's Fried Chicken in 1988. Around 1991, the space became Cobblestone Shoe Repair and then Golden Fried Chicken around 1996. Around 2000, China Wok Express opened in the location and stayed open for many years until it's closure in 2023. The building was then demolished the same year and is now the site of 7 Brew Coffee.

Shipley Do-Nuts, 210 E Villa Maria Rd, Bryan

Opened in 1982, moving from 3310 S College Avenue, Bryan.

Courtesy of The Courier

The Captain's Half Shell Oyster Bar, 206 E Villa Maria Rd, Bryan

Opened in 1985 and became The Boat Restaurant around 2003. The Boat then closed in 2009 and became Shipwreck Grill.

Courtesy of The Battalion

Pizza Planet, 203 E Villa Maria Rd, Bryan

Opened in 1979 and offered pizza, spaghetti, and salad, along with a lunch buffet. Pizza Planet closed in 1984 and the space became Kelley Moore Paint Company in 1985 and closed shortly after. In 1991, Beetle's BBQ moved into the space and closed in 1994. The same year, a short-lived Buffalo Joe's Restaurant opened and closed after a few months. Since then, it has been several other businesses until Amico Nave Ristorante opened in 2013 and became popular for its upscale Italian dining. Amico Nave eventually closed in 2024.

7-Eleven, 3300 Finfeather Rd, Bryan

Courtesy of The Eagle

Opened in 1978 and became an E-Z Mart in 1993. E-Z Mart then renamed to E-Z For You in the 2000s and is still open today.

Aerofit Health & Fitness Center, 1900 W Villa Maria Rd, Bryan

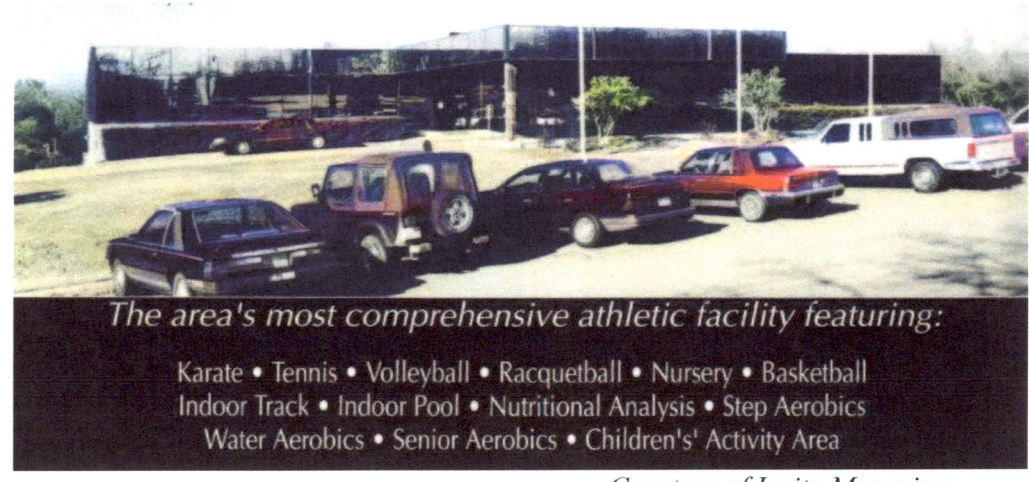

Courtesy of Insite Magazine

Opened in 1984 and became a Tru Fit Athletic Club in 2017.

Texas Hall of Fame, 649 N Harvey Mitchell Pkwy Bryan

Courtesy of YKYFBCS

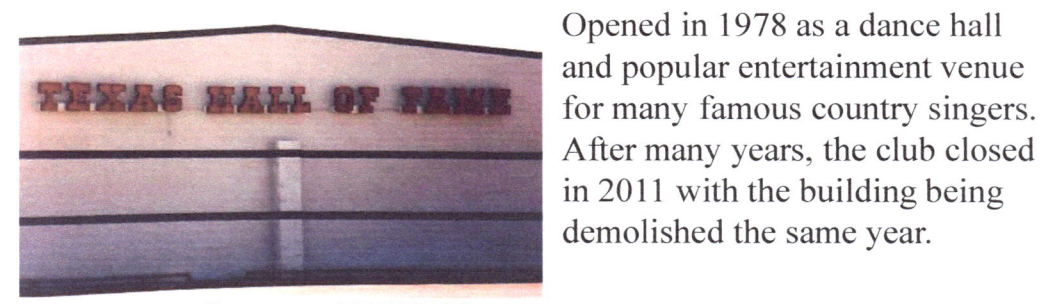

Courtesy of YKYFBCS

Opened in 1978 as a dance hall and popular entertainment venue for many famous country singers. After many years, the club closed in 2011 with the building being demolished the same year.

7-Eleven, 1296 N Harvey Mitchell Pkwy, Bryan

Courtesy of The Eagle

Opened in 1977 and became an E-Z Mart in 1993. E-Z Mart then closed in 2020 and the space has since been vacant.

Chapter 12: Finfeather Road, Bryan

Villa Maria & Finfeather Road Intersection, Bryan, 1982

Courtesy of Kovak & Co. Real Estate

Village Oaks Apartments,
3200 Finfeather Rd

Courtesy of The Eagle

Time Mart, 2626 Finfeather Rd, Bryan

Opened in the early 80s.

Courtesy of Google Earth

Courtesy of Kovak & Co. Real Estate

Peppertree Drive Apartments seen around 1988

Chapter 12: South College Avenue, Bryan

Shipley Do-Nuts, 3310 S College Avenue, Bryan

Courtesy of Project HOLD

Opened around 1955 as the first Shipley Do-Nuts in the area, and moved to 210 E Villa Maria Rd, Bryan in 1982.

The Texan Restaurant, 3204 S College Avenue, Bryan

Courtesy of The Eagle

Courtesy of The Eagle

Opened in 1967 and became a landmark in Bryan, offering gourmet dinner and fine dining. After many years, The Texan closed in 2000 due to the competition of other new restaurants. The building has since been used for other businesses throughout years.

7-Eleven, 3201 S College Avenue, Bryan

Courtesy of The Eagle

Opened in 1979 and became an E-Z Mart in 1993. E-Z Mart then became a Zip'N around 2003 and is still open today.

Tom's Barbeque, 3610 S College Avenue, Bryan

Courtesy of Bryan-College Station Visitors' Guide

Opened in 1985 and became J. Cody's Steak and Barbeque in 2001.

Youngblood's, 3410 S College Avenue, Bryan

Courtesy of The Eagle

Opened in 1946 and became a staple restaurant in the area, serving what locals claimed to be the best chicken fried steak in BCS. Youngbloods eventually closed in 1987 and the space became Carney's Pub, which is still open today.

Chapter 13: University Drive West & Northgate, College Station

Gulf Station, 420 S Texas Avenue, College Station

Courtesy of Cushing Memorial Library

Courtesy of The Eagle

Opened in the early 70s (seen on left) and remodeled in the late 70s into an orange-colored building. The gas station then became a Chevron in 1989 and eventually closed in the early 2000s. The building was then demolished in 2005 and is now the site of Northpoint Crossing apartments.

Courtesy of Cushing Memorial Library

Courtesy of Cushing Memorial Library

Kettle Restaurant, 1403 University Dr W, College Station

Courtesy of The Eagle

Courtesy of Gregory Gammon Photography

Opened in 1979 and closed in 2005. The building was then demolished for Northpoint Crossing Apartments in 2012.

Courtesy of Cushing Memorial Library

U Tote M, 1405 University Dr W, College Station

Courtesy of Kovak & Co. Real Estate

Opened around 1966 and became a Circle K in 1984 and closed shortly after in 1985. The space was used for several other businesses including a tobacco store before it was demolished in 2012. It is now the site of Northpoint Crossing Apartments.

Courtesy of Cushing Memorial Library *Courtesy of Cushing Memorial Library*
Sign can be seen

Skaggs Alpha Beta, 301 S College Avenue, College Station

Courtesy of Cushing Memorial Library

Opened in 1971 as Skaggs Albertsons and renamed to Skaggs Alpha Beta in 1979. The store then became a Jewel Osco in 1991 and then an Albertsons in 1992. In 1997, Albertsons moved to 615 University Dr E, College Station and the building was left vacant for many years. In 2012, the building was demolished and is now the site of The Stack Fields.

Courtesy of Sterling C. Evans Library

Hoffbrau Steaks Restaurant, 317 College Avenue, College Station

Courtesy of Project HOLD

Originally opened as Bonanza Steak House in 1973 and became WG & Company Restaurant in 1976. Hoffbrau then opened in 1982 and closed in 1985. In 1993, the space became The Cow Hop Restaurant (which also had a location in Northgate) and closed in 1996. Since then, the building has been used for several restaurants throughout the years.

Courtesy of The Eagle

Courtesy of The Battalion

Mr. Gatti's, 107 College Avenue, College Station

Courtesy of Cushing Memorial Library

Opened in 1974 and closed in 1998. The building was then demolished the same year for a Schlotzsky's, which is still open today.

IHOP, 103 College Avenue, College Station

Opened in 1974 as the area's first IHOP and eventually closed in 2024.

Courtesy of Insite Magazine

Cinema III, 313 College Avenue, College Station

Courtesy of Cushing Memorial Library

Opened in 1973 and added a third theater in 1983, renaming to Cinema III. The theater closed in 1995 due to competition from Hollywood USA theater (now Cinemark), and the Schulman 6 in Bryan.

Courtesy of The Eagle

725 University Dr, College Station

Courtesy of The Battalion
Inside of Music Express

Courtesy of The Battalion

Courtesy of Google Earth

Courtesy of Cushing Memorial Library

Originally housed Music Express (opened in 1980) and Tommy's Game Room (Opened in 1984). Tommy's Game Room then became Fat Burger in 1986 and Music Express closed around 1989. Fat Burger stayed open for many years until its closure in 2012, as the strip mall was demolished the same year. It is now the site of The Stack Fields.

Kinko's, 201 College Main St, College Station

Opened in 1979 and moved to 509 University Dr, College Station in 1989. That location then became FedEx around 2008.

Courtesy of Csroadsandretail.blogspot.com

Courtesy of The Eagle

115

111 University Dr, College Station

Courtesy of Insite Magazine

Opened in 1962 as College Station State Bank, the first bank in College Station. The space was used for several other banks throughout the years, including BB&T (seen below) before being demolished in 2016. It is now the site of The Rise at Northgate Apartments.

Courtesy of Google Earth

McDonald's, 801 University Dr, College Station

Courtesy of Gregory Gammon Photography *Courtesy of The Eagle*

Opened in 1973 and remodeled in the 80s (top-right picture). The restaurant then went through a few other remodels and got a more modern look in 2007.

Inside seen in the 80s

601 University Dr, College Station

Courtesy of Google Earth

Opening in 1987, this strip of restaurants originally housed a Baskin Robbins 31 Treats, Little Caesars, and Subway.

Courtesy of The Eagle  *Courtesy of Sterling C. Evans Library*

Greyhound Station, 112 Nagle St, College Station

Opened in 1976 and moved to 114 E Walton Dr, College Station in the mid 80s.

Courtesy of Cushing Memorial Library

117

Pizza Hut, 501 University Dr W, College Station

Courtesy of Project HOLD

Courtesy of Sterling C. Evans Library

Opened in 1982 and eventually closed in 1994. Aggieland Credit Union then opened in the space in 1995.

Courtesy of Project HOLD

Charlie's Grocery, 321 University Dr

Texas Aggie Book Store, 327 University Dr

Farmers Market Sandwich Shop, 329 University Dr

Loupot's Bookstore, 335 University Dr

Courtesy of Project HOLD

Courtesy of The Battalion

Courtesy of Csroadsandretail.blogspot.com

Northgate, College Station, 1986

Courtesy of The Battalion

From left to right: Sticky Chins Ice Cream, Dixie Chicken, Duddley's Draw, Wing Joint, & Cow Hop Restaurant.

303 University Dr, College Station

Courtesy of 1982 Texas A&M University Yearbook

Opened as The Alamo Restaurant & Bar in 1980 and became Bogie's Bar in 1983.

Courtesy of Project HOLD

The space then became Flying Tomato Pizza in 1985 and closed around 1991.

Patricia Street Shopping Center

Courtesy of Carnegie History Center

A small shopping center used to be located where the Boyett Street Parking Lot is now. The center opened in 1970 and was demolished in 1998 for the Northgate Revitalization Plan, which provided more parking and walkability for pedestrians.

U Tote M, 301 Patricia St

Courtesy of The Battalion

Opened around 1970 and closed in 1984.

7-Eleven, 301 University Dr, College Station

Courtesy of The Battalion

Opened around 1983 and became an E-Z Mart in 1993 (seen below). E-Z Mart then became Aggie Food Mart around 2005 and then Gig'em Food Mart in 2016. The gas station was eventually demolished in 2022.

Courtesy of Project HOLD

The Deluxe Diner, 203 University Dr, College Station

Photo: Rhonda Brinkmann
This 50s-style diner serves up delicious burgers, breakfasts and more!
Courtesy of The Battalion

Opened in 1983 and closed in 2006. The building was then demolished in 2012 and Chimy's Restaurant was built at the site in 2013.

Campus Theater, 217 University Dr, College Station

Courtesy of YKYFBCS

The Campus Theater opened in 1940 and was a popular venue for Texas A&M students for many decades. The theater eventually closed in 1985 and has since been the site of many nightclubs.

DoubleDave's Pizzaworks, 211 University Dr, College Station

Courtesy of Project HOLD

Opened in 1985 and closed in 2000.

123

4410 College Main St, College Station

Courtesy of The Battalion

Opened in 1978 as Grin's Beer Garden and became Dr. G's in 1983. Dr. G's was then replaced by Morgenstern's in 1986. In 1989, Brazos Landing, a restaurant in Northgate, replaced Morgenstern's and renamed as the Texas Star Tavern. The Texas Star Tavern closed shortly after, and the space became the Front Porch Café in 1990. Since 1992, the location has been Junction 505, a nonprofit organization.

Courtesy of The Battalion

Courtesy of The Battalion

Courtesy of The Battalion

Courtesy of The Battalion

Brazos Landing, Northgate

La Taqueria, 102 Church Avenue, College Station

Courtesy of The Battalion

Courtesy of Kovak & Co. Real Estate

Opened in 1984 and closed in 1991, turning into the Planetary Grub and Organic Juice Bar. The space then became La Bodega Baja Taco Bar in 2000 and eventually closed in 2014. The building was then demolished and now sits as an empty lot.

Café Eccell, 101 Church Avenue, College Station

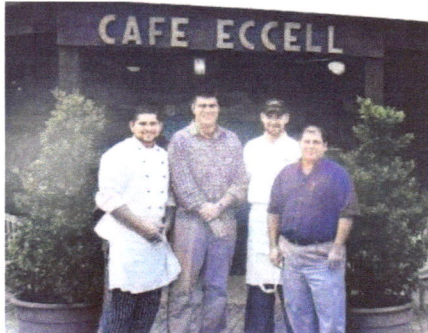

Courtesy of Google Earth *Courtesy of Insite Magazine*

Opened in 1989 and moved to 4401 S Texas Avenue, College Station in 2014. The building was then demolished and is now the site of the Domain at Northgate Apartments.

125

Chapter 14: Wellborn Road, College Station

Wellborn Rd, College Station

Courtesy of The Eagle

Finfeather and Villa Maria Rd, Bryan

An underpass was built at the intersection in 2008 and Finfeather now runs above Villa Maria Road.

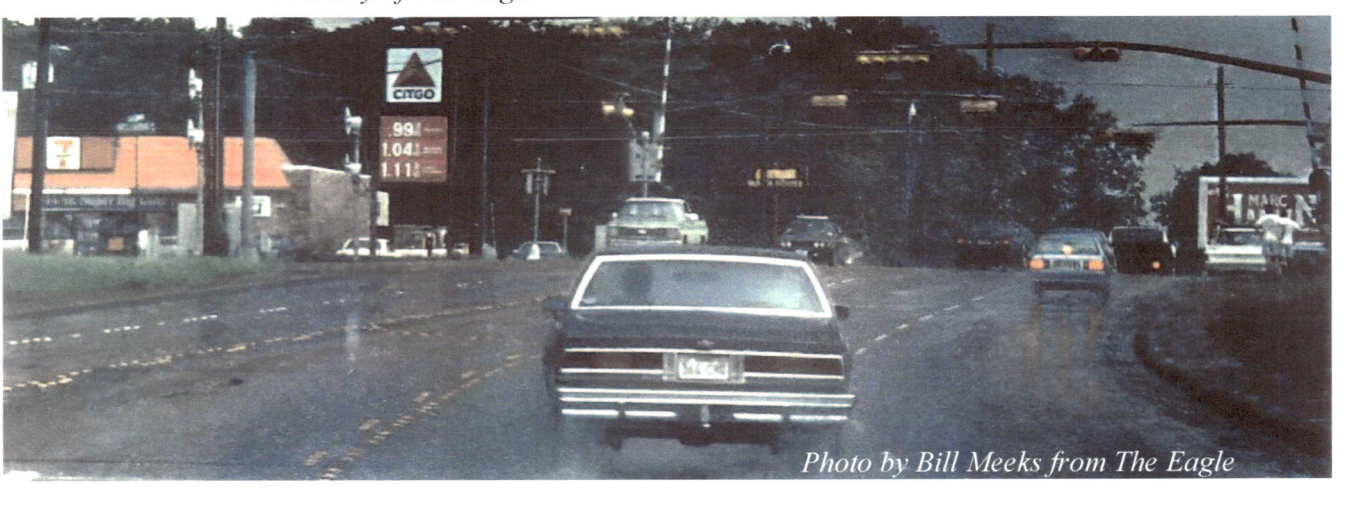

Photo by Bill Meeks from The Eagle

Texas A&M University Pedestrian Overpass

Courtesy of Cushing Memorial Library

Courtesy of Texags.com

Courtesy of YKYFBCS

Opened in 1974 and was used for pedestrians to cross Wellborn Road to main campus for many years. The bridge was demolished in 2001 and is now the site of Pickard Pass, which opened in 2003.

Fish Richards, 801 Wellborn Rd, College Station

Courtesy of The Eagle

Opened in 1978 from a converted home and became popular in the area for its seafood and fine dining. The restaurant also had a bar and lunch menu that served sandwiches, soups, and salad. Fish Richards eventually closed in 1986 and the house sat vacant until a fire destroyed the building in 1988. Since then, it was the site of an empty lot until the Berkley House apartments were built in 2018.

Courtesy of The Battalion
Fence outside Fish Richards

Courtesy of The Eagle
Dining area and bar can be seen

Chinese Fast Food Restaurant, 805 Wellborn Rd, College Station

Courtesy of Google Earth

Opened in 1985 as a part of Sing Lee Chinese Restaurant, which was located at 3030 East 29th St, Bryan. The fast-food restaurant was in a former convenience store (seen above) and offered buffet style food. The restaurant closed around 1990 but the convenience store stayed open for many years until it was demolished for Berkley House apartments in 2017.

Owner Shirley Peng inside Chinese Fast Food Restaurant

Courtesy of The Eagle

Judd's Food Store, 1011 Wellborn Rd, College Station

Courtesy of Carnegie History Center

Opened in 1989 and became a Valero Station in the mid 2000s. The gas station was then demolished in 2020 and a McDonald's was built at the site in 2023.

C.C. Creations, 114 Holleman Dr, College Station

Courtesy of Carnegie History Center

Opened in 1988

Chapter 15: George Bush Drive, College Station

Rother's Bookstore, 340 George Bush Dr, College Station

Courtesy of Project HOLD

Opened in 1978 and closed around 2003. The space then became Traditions Bookstore in the mid 2000s and closed around 2013. It is now the site of Fidelis Creative Agency.

DoubleDave's Pizzaworks, 330 George Bush Dr, College Station

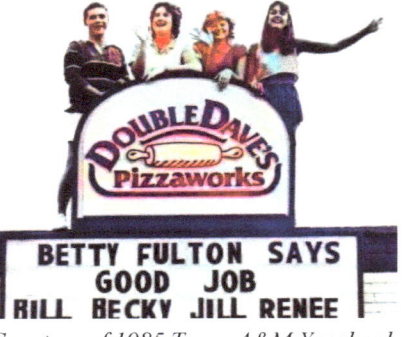

Courtesy of 1985 Texas A&M Yearbook

Opened in 1984 as the first established DoubleDave's and eventually closed in 2001.

Circle K, 208 George Bush Dr, College Station

Courtesy of Cushing Memorial Library

Originally a Sak-N-Pak store, it became a U Tote M around 1977 and then a Circle K in 1984. Circle K then closed in 1993 and the space became a Tropicana convenience store seen below. The store closed in 2001 and the building was demolished for an Aggieland Outfitters in 2002.

Courtesy of Cushing Memorial Library

George Bush Drive, College Station, 1986

Courtesy of Cushing Memorial Library

133

Chapter 16: University Drive East, College Station

Sigmor Shamrock Gas Station, 501 Texas Avenue, College Station

Courtesy of Cushing Memorial Library

Courtesy of Project HOLD

Opened in the early 70s as a Fill-em Fast Station and became a Sigmor Shamrock in 1978. Sigmor then renamed to Diamond Shamrock in 1989 (seen on right) and a small convenience store was built next to the pumps. Diamond Shamrock closed around 1998 and the space became a U-Haul around 1999.

Courtesy of Cushing Memorial Library

Sonic Drive-In, 104 University Dr E

Pizza Hut, 102 University Dr

Courtesy of Cushing Memorial Library

Opened in 1973 as the first Sonic in College Station and closed around 2003. In 2007 the building was demolished, and a Brake Check Service Center was built at the site.

Opened in 1974 as the second Pizza Hut in the area and eventually closed in 2017. The building's parking lot is now used for Fuego Tortilla Grill, located at 108 Poplar St.

Hi-Lo Auto Supply, 210 University Dr, College Station

Courtesy of Cushing Memorial Library

Courtesy of Cushing Memorial Library

Opened in 1977 and became O'Reilly Auto Parts around 1998.

Egg Roll House, 200 University Dr E, College Station

Courtesy of Cushing Memorial Library

Opened in 1977 and offered fast Chinese food at lower prices. Egg Roll House eventually closed in 1996 and the building sat vacant for many years. The building was eventually demolished in 2009 and a Jimmy John's was built the same year.

404 Center, 404 University Dr E, College Station

Courtesy of Insite Magazine

100,000 Auto Parts, 402 University Dr E, College Station

Courtesy of Project HOLD

Opened in 1972 and closed in 1988, becoming Carquest Auto Parts. Carquest then closed in 2014 and is now the site of NAPA Auto Parts.

505 Center, 505 University Dr E, College Station

Courtesy of Cushing Memorial Library

Opened in 1980 and remodeled around 2020.

Randy's Liquor, 524 University Dr E, College Station

Courtesy of Cushing Memorial Library

Courtesy of The Battalion

Courtesy of The Battalion
Dave's Liquor Sign

Opened in 1972 as Randy's Liquor and became Dave's Liquor in 1985. Dave's Liquor then closed around 1991 and the space became Audio Video in 1994. The building was then demolished the same year and is now the site of 522 University Dr Center.

The Grapevine Restaurant, 201 Live Oak St, College Station

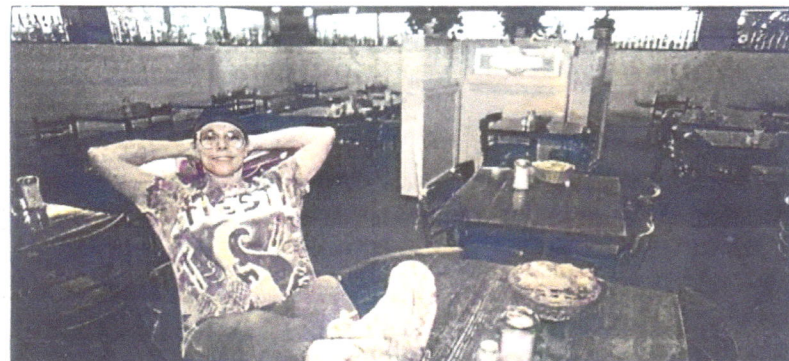

Photo by Dave McDermand from The Eagle

Opened in 1981 by owner Patsy Zabel (seen on right). The restaurant became a staple in the area, known for its twice baked potatoes, salads, and wine. The Grapevine eventually closed in 2001 and is now the site of Rohr Chabad Jewish Center at Texas A&M University.

University Drive East, College Station, 1982

Courtesy of Cushing Memorial Library

FedMart, 701 University Dr E, College Station

Courtesy of Project HOLD

Courtesy of Project HOLD

Courtesy of The Eagle

Opened in 1973 as a discount department store with an auto service center. The store closed shortly after in 1981, and the building was demolished for Chimney Hill Shopping Center in 1984. The Auto Service Center was left and was turned into the Bryan-College Station Chamber of Commerce the same year.

Chimney Hill Shopping Center, 701 University Dr E, College Station

Courtesy of Google Earth

Bowl sign can be seen

Courtesy of Texashistory.unt.edu

Opened in 1984 along with a bowling center. The shopping center was open for many years until the 2010s, as stores started to move out and the center became vacant. In 2016, Chimney Hill was torn down, and the site now houses individual restaurants such as The Republic Steakhouse, Five Guys, Starbucks, and Snooze, an A.M. Eatery.

Opened in 1984 as Confederate House Restaurant and renamed to Tradition in 1985. Tradition eventually closed in 1987.

Courtesy of Csroadsandretail.blogspot.com

Pacific Garden Restaurant opened in 1986 and closed in 1991.

Courtesy of The Eagle

Courtesy of The Battalion

143

The Village Shopping Center, 700 University Dr E, College Station

Courtesy of Insite Magazine

Opened in 1984

University Drive Water Tower

Courtesy of Project HOLD

Constructed in the early 70s and was demolished around 2003. It is now the site of College Station Fire Department Station 6.

Hilton Hotel, 801 University Dr E, College Station

Courtesy of YKYFBCS

Opened in 1985

Courtesy of The Battalion

K-Bob's Steakhouse, Creekside Retail Plaza, College Station

Courtesy of Insite Magazine

Opened in 1985 and closed in 1991.

Scott & White Clinic, 1600 University Dr E, College Station

Courtesy of Insite Magazine

Opened in 1986 and closed in 2015. The building was then demolished in 2016 and now sits as a vacant lot.

Chapter 17: Earl Rudder Freeway, College Station

Lowe's, 2400 Earl Rudder Fwy, College Station

Courtesy of YKYFBCS

Opened in 1986 as the area's first Lowe's and closed shortly after in 1987. The building was then turned into Wolf Pen Bowl and Skate in 1990 and eventually closed in 2007. In 2008, the space became Grand Station Entertainment, which offers bowling, laser tag, and mini golf.

Wolf Pen Bowl and Skate

Courtesy of City of Bryan Flickr

147

Stephen C. Beachy Central Park,
1000 Krenek Tap Rd, College Station

Courtesy of YKYFBCS

Opened in 1979

Courtesy of City of College Station YouTube

Allen Honda, 2450 Earl Rudder Fwy S, College Station

Courtesy of 1986 Bryan High School Yearbook

Courtesy of The Eagle

Opened in 1985 and remodeled in 2002.

148

Chapter 18: Texas Avenue South, College Station

Texas Avenue South, College Station, 1982

Julie's Place, 607 Texas Avenue, College Station

Courtesy of Cushing Memorial Library

Photo by Peter Rocha from The Eagle

Opened in 1978 as a homestyle cooking restaurant and became Bombay Bicycle Club Restaurant in 1988. Bombay Bicycle Club featured a sports bar, hot-food bar, and salad bar. The restaurant eventually closed in 1996 and Denny's Restaurant opened the same year.

Courtesy of Cushing Memorial Library

Texas 707 Center, 707 Texas Avenue, College Station

Courtesy of Insite Magazine

Opened in 1974 and in 1997, a portion of the center was demolished for an On The Border Restaurant.

Pasta's Pizza, 807 Texas Avenue, College Station

Courtesy of Cushing Memorial Library

Originally an Oakridge Smokehouse, it became Pasta's Pizza in 1979 and closed in 1985. Las Palmas Mexican restaurant then opened at the site in 1986 and closed shortly after in 1987. The space then became Ladies & Lords Clothing Store in 1991 and moved to Eastgate in 1997. The building was then demolished the same year for an On The Border Restaurant.

Taco Cabana, 701 Texas Avenue, College Station

Courtesy of 1992 Texas A&M University Yearbook

Opened in 1988 and closed in 2020.

Red Lobster, 813 Texas Avenue, College Station

Courtesy of Project HOLD

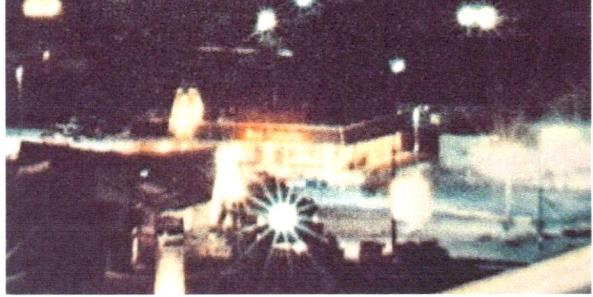

Courtesy of Insite Magazine

Courtesy of Google Earth

Opened in 1983 and moved to 1200 University Dr E, College Station in 2008. In 2013, Lupe Tortilla opened in the location.

819 Texas Avenue, College Station

Courtesy of Blog.cstx.gov

Originally a real estate office, the space became Computer Access in 1988 and then BCS Bicycles in 1991. BCS Bicycles then closed in the mid 90s and the space became Soulworks Art Gallery & Gift Shop in 1999. Soulworks closed in 2003 and the building was demolished around 2005 for a T-Mobile Store.

Courtesy of Cushing Memorial Library

Eastgate Live, 109 Walton Dr, College Station

Courtesy of The Battalion *Courtesy of Eastgate Live !! Facebook Page*

Courtesy of Eastgate Live !! Facebook Page

Opened in 1985 as MC² Club (seen in top-left picture), which featured electronic/new wave music. MC² moved to 815 Harvey Rd in 1986 and the space became Eastgate Live the same year. Eastgate Live hosted live bands with a variety of music from classic rock, blues, to reggae. The club eventually closed in 1989 and has been the site of different businesses throughout the years.

Acme Glass Co, 116 Walton Dr, College Station

Courtesy of Carnegie History Center

Opened in 1973

U Tote M, 105 Walton Dr, College Station

Courtesy of The Eagle

Opened in 1961 and became a Circle K in 1984. Circle K then became Eastgate Food Store in 1986. In the early 2000s, the space became Military Depot.

Mama's Pizza, 1037 Texas Avenue S, College Station

Courtesy of YKYFBCS

Originally Couch Norton's Pancake House, and then Fontana's Restaurant, the space became Mama's Pizza in 1979. Mama's Pizza eventually closed in 1991, and the space was used for several other restaurants throughout the years. It is now the site of Torchy's Tacos.

Courtesy of The Battalion

Sambo's Restaurant, 1045 Texas Avenue S, College Station

Courtesy of Gregory Gammon Photography

Courtesy of Cushing Memorial Library

Opened in 1974 and became Wings 'N Things in 1988. The restaurant then renamed to Wings 'N More in 1990 and eventually moved to 1511 University Dr E, College Station in 2002. In 2005, the building was demolished and is now the site of Raising Cane's (opened in 2006).

Courtesy of Bryan-College Station Visitors' Guide

Redmond Terrace Center, 1400 Texas Avenue, College Station

Date: 1986

Courtesy of Cushing Memorial Library

Opened in 1964 was demolished in 2003 for a new building.

Redmond Terrace Center, College Station

Academy Sports & Outdoors, 1420 Texas Avenue S

Photo by Bill Meeks from The Eagle

Courtesy of Sterling C. Evans Library

Opened in 1983 and moved to 2351 Earl Rudder Fwy, College Station in 2001. That location then closed in 2017 and moved to a larger building at 2511 Earl Rudder Fwy, College Station.

Engineering & Office Supply

Courtesy of Insite Magazine

Opened in 1979 and closed in 1997.

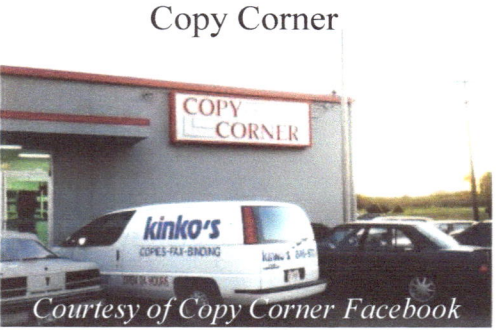

Copy Corner

Courtesy of Copy Corner Facebook

Opened in 1988 and moved to 2307 Texas Avenue S, College Station in 2004.

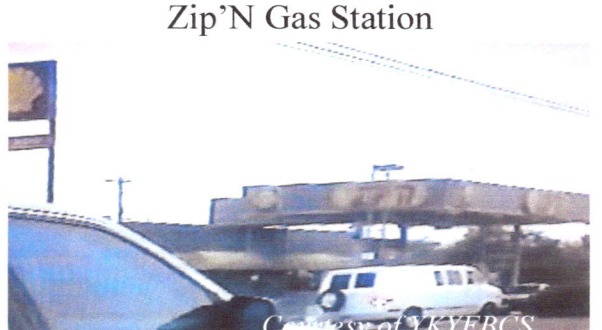

Zip'N Gas Station

Courtesy of YKYFBCS

Opened in 1986, replacing a former Amoco Gas Station. The building was then torn down in 2003 to make way for the renovated Redmond Terrace Center.

157

Brown's Shoe Fit, Redmond Terrace Center, College Station

Courtesy of The Battalion

Opened in 1982 and moved to 2553 Texas Ave S, College Station in 2002.

Amoco Station, 1400 Texas Avenue S, College Station

Opened in the early 60s (seen below) and remodeled in the mid 80s. It then became Zip'N Gas Station in 1986.

Courtesy of Cushing Memorial Library

Courtesy of Cushing Memorial Library

Courtesy of 1980 A&M Consolidated High School Yearbook

Texaco Station, 1405 Texas Avenue, College Station

Courtesy of Google Earth

Courtesy of The Eagle

Originally Zulkowski's Texaco (seen on left) and became an H&M Texaco Food Mart in 1985. This renamed to Max Texaco in the early 90s and closed in the early 2000s. The building was then demolished in 2007 and is now an empty lot.

Whataburger, 105 Dominik Dr, College Station

Courtesy of The Courier

Courtesy of Cushing Memorial Library

Courtesy of Cushing Memorial Library

Opened in 1986 as a remodel of the original drive in (seen on left). The remodel lasted until 1996 when the building burned down and was remodeled again.

Danver's, 201 Dominik Dr, College Station

Courtesy of 1980 A&M Consolidated High School Yearbook

Opened in 1978 and closed around 1985. The space then became the Texas Aggie Bookstore in 1987 and then the Brazos Brewing Company in 1995. In 1998, the Brazos Blue Ribbon Bakery moved into the location and closed shortly after, becoming a Blue Baker in 2001.

Quick as a Flash, 110 Dominik Dr, College Station

Photo by Bill Meeks from The Eagle

Opened in 1987 replacing a former Kentucky Fried Chicken. The space is now Shiraz Shish Kabob.

Courtesy of 1993 A&M Consolidated High School Yearbook

Culpepper Plaza, 1505 Texas Avenue S, College Station

Bennigan's, 1505A Texas Avenue S

Courtesy of Osborn & Vane Architects, Inc

Opened in 1982 and closed in 2009. AT&T then opened in the space the same year.

Swensen's Ice Cream, 1507 Texas Avenue S

Courtesy of Osborn & Vane Architects, Inc

Opened in 1979 and closed in 2005.

Courtesy of The Eagle *Courtesy of 1979 Texas A&M Yearbook*

161

Culpepper Plaza, College Station

Weiner's, 1661 Texas Avenue S

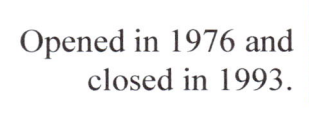

Opened in 1976 and closed in 1993.

Courtesy of Cushing Memorial Library

Eckerd Drugs, 1701 Texas Avenue S

Courtesy of Insite Magazine

3C Barbeque, 1727 Texas Avenue S

Opened in 1976 and closed in the early 90s.

Courtesy of The Battalion

Courtesy of Cushing Memorial Library

Opened in 1976 and closed in the mid 90s.

Culpepper Plaza, College Station

Texas Tumbleweed, 1521 Texas Avenue S

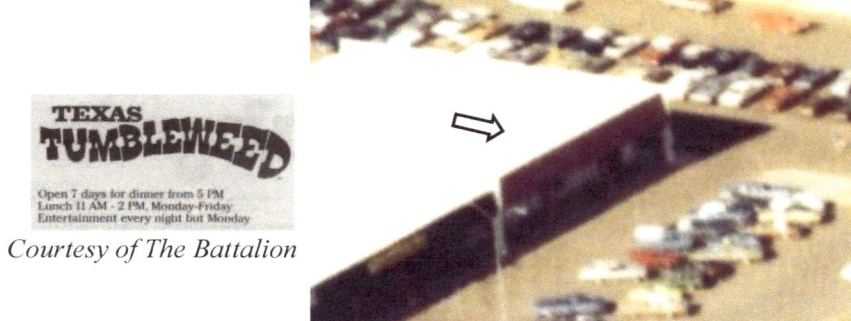

Courtesy of The Battalion

Courtesy of Cushing Memorial Library

Table seen at Texas Tumbleweed

Courtesy of 1983 A&M Consolidated High School Yearbook

Opened in 1982 (replacing a former Rosewood Junction Restaurant) and was a steakhouse restaurant that offered live entertainment. Texas Tumbleweed closed in 1987 and the space became Cow Hop Junction in 1988 and then Pancho's Mexican Buffet in 1992 (which remodeled the building). In 1999, Los Cucos Mexican Café opened in the space and the building was remodeled again in 2006.

Courtesy of The Eagle

The building's different faces from Pancho's to Los Cucos (on right).

Courtesy of Carnegie History Center

Culpepper Plaza, College Station

Hastings Books, Music and Video

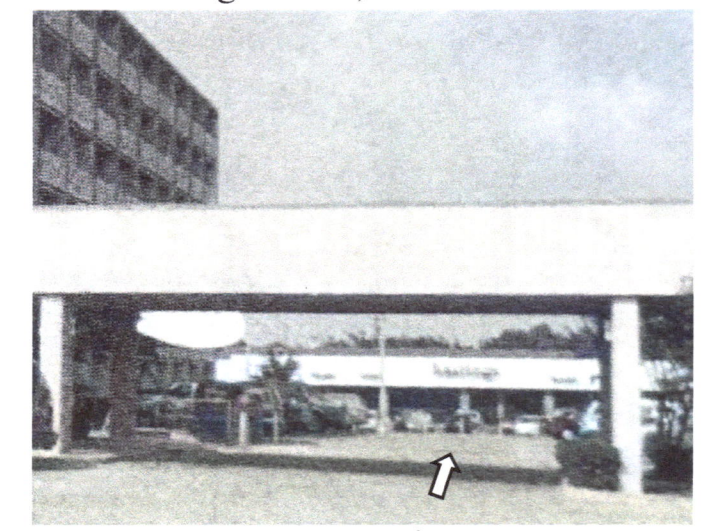

Courtesy of Insite Magazine

Opened in 1979 and moved in to 2004 Texas Avenue S, College Station in 1995. That location then closed in 2015.

Burger King, 1719 Texas Avenue S

Courtesy of Project HOLD   *Courtesy of Osborn & Vane Architects, Inc*

Courtesy of Project HOLD

Opened in 1985 and closed in 2007. The building was demolished the same year for a Chick-Fil-A.

Safeway, Culpepper Plaza, College Station

AppleTree Store

Courtesy of Cushing Memorial Library

Courtesy of The Eagle

Courtesy of The Battalion

Opened in 1976 and became an AppleTree in 1989. AppleTree then closed in 2002 and the building was remodeled in 2006. In 2007, Spec's Wines, Spirits & Finer Foods opened in the location.

Courtesy of Kovak & Co. Real Estate

Texas Avenue South, seen in 1993

Courtesy of Project HOLD

Pilger's Exxon Station,
1721 Texas Avenue S, College Station

Courtesy of Cushing Memorial Library

Opened in the early 70s offering a service center and gas station. Pilger's Station closed in the late 90s and the building was demolished for a Speedy Stop in 2000. Speedy Stop then became a Tetco Station in 2013 and then a 7-Eleven around 2022.

Chapter 19: Harvey Road, College Station

J.J. Muggs Restaurant & Bar, 1704 George Bush Dr E, College Station

Courtesy of Archive.org

Courtesy of Archive.org

Opened in 1984 and closed in 1987. Rita's Eaterie & Cantina then opened in 1988 (seen in photos) and became Garcia's Mexican Café in 1992. Garcia's then closed in 2002 and the space became Fuddruckers in 2003. Fuddruckers eventually closed in 2020 and is now the site of iWon Korean BBQ & Hot Pot.

Courtesy of The Battalion

Thomas Sweet, 1702 George Bush Dr E, College Station

Courtesy of The Eagle

Opened in 1985 and closed in 1989.

1702 Kyle South (behind J.J. Muggs) College Station

Courtesy of The Battalion

Cashion Cain Christmas Store, 504 Harvey Rd, College Station

Courtesy of The Battalion

Opened in 1984 and sold Christmas decorations, dinnerware, and household accessories. Cashion Cain closed in 1989 and the space then became Sneakers Club the same year. Sneakers had a dance floor, pool tables, lounge area, and an outdoor volleyball court for matches. Sneakers closed shortly after in 1992 and the building was eventually demolished for Rudy's Barbeque in 2000.

Archie's Taco Bell, 310 Harvey Rd, College Station

Photo by Butch Ireland from The Eagle

Opened in 1982 and remodeled in the early 2000s.

View of Harvey Road in 1992

Courtesy of Kovak & Co. Real Estate

Courtesy of 1983 A&M Consolidated High School Yearbook

169

Woodstone Shopping Center, 909 Harvey Rd, College Station

Frank's Bar & Grill

T Shirts Plus & Athletic Attic

Archie's 39¢ Hamburger Place

Courtesy of The Eagle

Courtesy of The Eagle

Courtesy of The Battalion

Courtesy of Blinn College

Woodstone Shopping Center opened in 1977.

170

Woodstone Shopping Center

814 Harvey Rd

Courtesy of The Eagle

Courtesy of The Battalion

Opened in 1977 as the C&S Transit Co. Restaurant and became Beef & Brew Restaurant in 1980. Since then, the building was used for several clubs throughout the 80s until The Tap bar opened in 1991, which is still open today.

Zephyr Club, 913A Harvey

Courtesy of The Battalion

Opened in 1982 as a rock 'n' roll club, which featured live music and an outdoor patio with full-service bar. The club closed in 1992 and has been the site of different businesses throughout the years.

171

Courtesy of The Eagle

Post Oak Village, 900 Harvey Rd, College Station

Courtesy of Kovak & Co. Real Estate

Opened in 1982 along with Post Oak Mall.

Courtesy of The Eagle

Post Oak Square, 1100 Harvey Rd, College Station

Opened in 1983

Aerial view from 1986

Courtesy of Insite Magazine

Cavender's Boot City, 1400 Harvey Rd

Courtesy of Project HOLD

Opened in 1987 and moved to 2300 Earl Rudder Fwy S, College Station in 2004. The building was then demolished around 2014 and now sits as an empty lot behind the Mattress Sleep Centers store.

Post Oak Square, College Station

Grandy's, 1002 E Harvey Rd

Imperial Restaurant, 1102 Harvey Rd

Courtesy of The Eagle

Courtesy of The Eagle

Opened in 1983 and closed in 1992. The building was then demolished in the early 90s and is now the site of Krispy Kreme Donuts.

Courtesy of The Eagle

Opened in 1984 and moved to 2232 Texas Avenue S, College Station in 1994. Ninfa's Mexican Restaurant then opened in 1995 and eventually closed in 2008. The space then became Wolfies Restaurant & Sports Bar from 2012 to 2016. And in 2018, Gumby's Pizza opened in the location.

Photo by Peter Rocha from The Eagle

Courtesy of Carnegie History Center

Post Oak Square, College Station

Weingarten's, 1200 Harvey Rd

Photo by Dave McDermand from The Eagle

Opened in 1983 and closed shortly after in 1984 becoming Mariel's Fine Foods. Mariel's then closed in 1985 and Hobby Lobby opened in the location in 1993. Hobby Lobby then moved to 1903 Texas Avenue S, College Station in 2001.

Courtesy of The Eagle

Mariel's FINE FOODS
Full Service Supermarket

"FLORAL DEPARTMENT"	"FULL SERVICE DELI"	"SCRATCH BAKERY"
Cut Flowers & Plants For All Occasions	We Cater! Party Trays And Instore Eating Area	French Pastries And All Occasion Cakes
"GIFT SHOP" Video Club, Jewelry, Small Appliances And Exclusive Fragrances	"CUSTOM CUT MEAT COUNTER" Specializing In Angus Beef As Well As Choice Also Fresh Seafood	"PRODUCE" Garden Fresh Produce
"FULL GOURMET LINES" Foods From Around The World Imported Wine		"WE DELIVER" If we sell it we'll deliver it!" Call in orders 8:00am to 12 noon delivered 12 noon to 1pm

We Accept VISA & MASTER CARD

1200 Harvey Road to East Bypass 6   College Station   764-9727

Courtesy of The Eagle

Post Oak Mall, 1500 Harvey Rd, College Station

Opened in 1982 (original exterior seen in photos) and remodeled in 1993 and again in 2013.

Photos are Courtesy of City of College Station YouTube

7-Eleven, 1401 Harvey Rd, College Station

Courtesy of Project HOLD

Opened in 1974 and became an E-Z Mart in 1993. E-Z Mart then renamed to E-Z Stop in 2001 and is still open today.

Jose's Restaurant, Highway 30, College Station

Originally the Crown and Anchor Inn, and then Karl's Restaurant, the space became Jose's Restaurant in 1978. Known for it's homestyle Mexican food, Jose's Restaurant was open for many years until 1993, when a fire destroyed the building. Jose's then moved to 3824 S Texas Avenue, Bryan the same year.

All photos are courtesy of Jose's Restaurant

Chapter 20: Holleman Drive, College Station

Jot 59 Laundry & Dry Cleaning,
103 Holleman Dr E

Courtesy of The Battalion

Courtesy of The Courier

Originally opened as Hank's Laundry & Dry Cleaning in 1979 and became Jot 59 in 1983, which is still open today.

Domino's,
1504 Holleman Dr

Courtesy of Domino's

Opened in 1978 and closed in 2002.

7-Eleven, 1500 Holleman Dr

Opened in 1974 and became Kelly's Corner Store around 1994. The space then became Shop N Go Food Mart in 2000 and is still open today.

Pizza Hut,
1103 Anderson St

Opened in 1984 as a delivery store and closed in 2004.

Chapter 21: Texas Avenue South, College Station Continued…

Aggieland Inn, 1502 Texas Avenue S, College Station

Jack in the Box, 1504 Texas Avenue S, College Station

Courtesy of Carnegie History Center  *Courtesy of The Battalion*

Courtesy of Gregory Gammon Photography

Opened in 1974 and became a Ramada Inn in 1988 and eventually closed in 2011. The main building was remodeled, and the lobby and restaurant were turned into a shopping center in 2016. The hotel opened as TRYP Wyndham in 2017 and became Aggieland Boutique Hotel in 2022.

Opened in 1976

J.J.'s Liquor, 1600 Texas Avenue S, College Station

Courtesy of YKYFBCS

Opened in 1972 as Discount Liquor and became J.J.'s in 1983. J.J.'s then closed around 2017 and the space became What's The Buzz Coffee in 2021. What's The Buzz then moved to 2511 S Texas Avenue, Bryan in 2023.

Zip'N Gas Station, 321 Redmond Dr, College Station

Courtesy of Loopnet.com

Dating back to the early 70s, this Shell Station became a Zip'N in 1986 and then Afnan Shell Station around 1990. Afnan Shell eventually closed in 2006 and the building was demolished the same year. The space sat as an empty lot until Aspen Dental was built in 2013.

Kashim Club, 1802 Texas Avenue, College Station

Courtesy of The Battalion   *Courtesy of The Battalion*

Kashim (the name of a gathering place used by Alaska natives), opened in 1975 and became a popular club for disco music and live entertainment. Kashim's eventually closed in 1983 and the building was demolished the same year. It is now the site of Harvey Washbangers.

Pepper's Hamburgers, 1808 Texas Avenue, College Station

Courtesy of The Eagle

Originally opened as Dairy Palace in 1977 and became Carter's Burgers shortly after (seen below). Ken Martin's Pepper's then opened in 1978 and offered hamburgers, chili, hot dogs, and soft tacos. Pepper's eventually closed in 1985 and the building was demolished the same year for a shopping center.

Long John Silver's, 1808 Texas Avenue, College Station

Opened in 1981 as the only Long John Silver's in College Station and eventually closed in 2006. The building was demolished the same year for a shopping center.

Courtesy of Project HOLD

Courtesy of The Battalion

**Tinsley's Chicken,
1905 Texas Avenue S, College Station**

Courtesy of Sterling C. Evans Library

Courtesy of Archive.org

Example of the building

Opened in 1979 next to Pooh's Park and closed in 1986. It is now the site of Wolf Pen Plaza.

Pooh's Park, 1907 Texas Avenue S, College Station

Courtesy of 1978 Bryan High School Yearbook

Courtesy of YKYFBCS

Opened in 1972 and became a popular skating rink and amusement park in the area. Pooh's Park eventually closed in 1986 and the building sat vacant for many years. In 2001, the building was eventually demolished for Wolf Pen Plaza, which houses a Hobby Lobby, Ross, and Big Lots.

Bud Ward Volkswagen, 1912 Texas Avenue S, College Station

Courtesy of The Eagle

Courtesy of The Eagle   *Courtesy of 1979 Bryan High School Yearbook*

Originally Richard Barton Volkswagen, it changed hands to Bud Ward in 1977. The dealership then became University Mitsubishi in 1989 and closed shortly after, as the building was demolished for El Chico Restaurant (opened in 1995). El Chico closed in 2005, and the building was demolished for MidSouth Bank, now Hancock Whitney Bank.

Texas Avenue South Water Tower, College Station

Courtesy of Project HOLD

Constructed in 1968 and was demolished in 2002.

185

Homecraft Electronics,
1921 Texas Avenue S, College Station

Courtesy of The Battalion

Opened in 1978 and closed around 1985.

Courtesy of The Battalion

Dave's Seafood & Steak Restaurant,
2001 Texas Avenue S, College Station

Courtesy of Bryan-College Station Visitors' Guide

Opened in 1984 as Dave's Seafood & Steak Restaurant and became Johnny Peppy's Restaurant and Lounge in 1985. In 1987, the space then became Karin's Restaurant before turning into Tom's Barbeque in 1991. Tom's Barbeque then closed in 2001 and the building was demolished in 2005 for a strip mall.

Texas Avenue South, College Station

Courtesy of Kovak & Co. Real Estate

Fuddruckers, 2206 Texas Avenue S, College Station

Courtesy of Kovak & Co. Real Estate

Opened in 1984 and moved to 1704 George Bush Dr E, College Station in 2003.

Courtesy of The Battalion

Courtesy of Texashistory.unt.edu

Courtesy of Texashistory.unt.edu

Courtesy of Texashistory.unt.edu

187

J.T. McCord's, 2232 Texas Avenue S, College Station

Opened in 1983 and closed in 1988. In 1994, the space became Imperial Chinese Restaurant, which moved from 1102 Harvey Rd, College Station. Imperial then closed in 2005 and College Station Pawn opened in 2006.

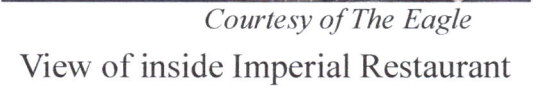

Courtesy of The Battalion

Imperial Restaurant

Courtesy of Kovak & Co. Real Estate

Courtesy of The Eagle
View of inside Imperial Restaurant

Courtesy of Kovak & Co. Real Estate
Sign can be seen

Confucius Chinese Cuisine, 2322 Texas Avenue S, College Station

College Station Pawn, 2316 Texas Avenue S

Courtesy of Maps.bryantx.gov

Courtesy of The Eagle

Courtesy of College Station Pawn Facebook

Courtesy of College Station Pawn Facebook

Photo by Peter Rocha from The Eagle
Sign on Texas Avenue

Opened in 1983 as Jade Garden Restaurant and became Confucius Chinese Cuisine in 1987. Owned by Jimmy Chang, (seen above) Confucius became a popular restaurant offering authentic Chinese food in a buffet style setting. After many years, Confucius closed in 2001 and the building was demolished the same year. A Walgreens was built at the site and took the space of the restaurant and College Station Pawn next door.

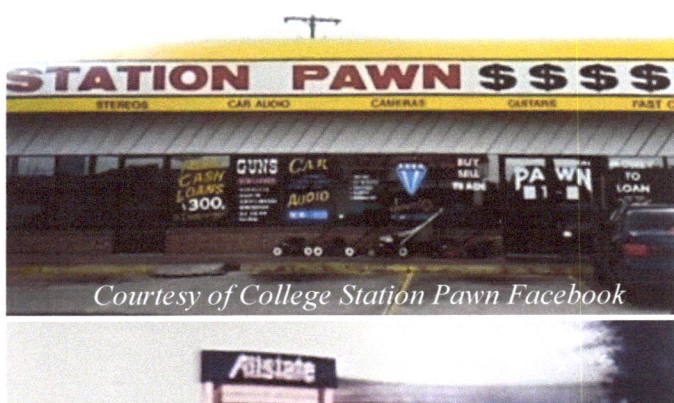

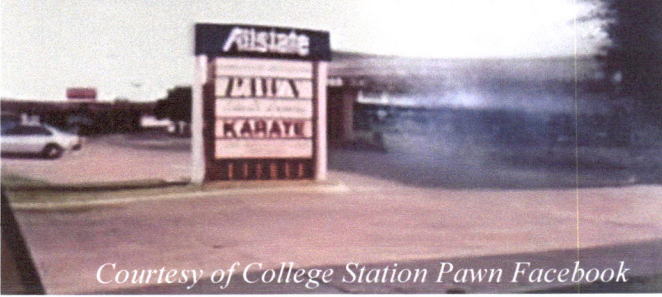

Opened in 1981 as Tops Office Products and became College Station Pawn in 1987.

Courtesy of The Battalion

189

Luther's Barbeque, 2319 Texas Avenue, S College Station

Motel 6, 2327 Texas Avenue S, College Station

Opened in 1985 and closed shortly after in 1986. Pop's Bar-B-Q then opened in the location 1989 and closed around 1992. In 1995, the space became Epicures Catering (seen on left) and eventually closed in 2011. The building has since been remodeled and is now Big O Tires.

Courtesy of Loopnet.com

Dairy Queen, 2323 Texas Avenue S, College Station

Opened in 1977 and remodeled around 2013.

Courtesy of Google Earth

Courtesy of The Eagle

Opened in 1980

Parkway Square, 2412 Texas Avenue S, College Station

Courtesy of Archive.org

Courtesy of The Eagle

Parkway Square opened in 1981 originally housing a Kroger Family Center, TG&Y, and many other stores. TG&Y closed shortly after in 1985 and the space was used for other businesses throughout the years. In 2001, Kroger remodeled from its greenhouse design (seen above) and eventually closed in 2016. It is now the site of TruFit Athetic Clubs, which opened in 2018.

Courtesy of The Eagle

Courtesy of Project HOLD

Courtesy of Carnegie History Center

Courtesy of 1991 A&M Consolidated High School Yearbook

Opened in 1982 Chuck E. Cheese's Pizza Time Theatre and closed shortly after in 1984. The space then became Kroger Family Center Video from 1991 to around 1997. It is now the site of Uptown Cheapskate clothing store.

Courtesy of 1991 A&M Consolidated High School Yearbook

McDonald's opened in 1981 and originally had an outdoor playground (seen in left picture) and the sign initially had golden arches. In 2004, the building was remodeled, and the playground was removed for an indoor play area which featured video game kiosks. In 2006, a tornado hit the area and blew the golden arches off the sign. The sign was left as is, and the building was remodeled again in 2019, giving it a more modern look.

Parkway Square, College Station

Courtesy of Archive.org

Courtesy of Archive.org

Courtesy of The Battalion

Courtesy of The Battalion

Courtesy of The Eagle

Courtesy of The Eagle

Old South Restaurant

Courtesy of The Eagle

Courtesy of The Battalion

Opened in 1982 and became BB's Oriental Restaurant in 1983. The space then became Old Country Buffet in 1994 and eventually closed in 2002, becoming China King Buffet. China King Buffet eventually closed in 2021.

Commerce National Bank,
2405 Texas Avenue S, College Station

Courtesy of Insite Magazine

Opened in 1984 and closed in 1997.
It is now the site of PNC Bank.

2411 Texas Avenue S, College Station

Courtesy of The Eagle

Became CarePlus Medical Center in 1992. The building was then torn down in 1998 for an Eckerd Drugs and became a CVS Pharmacy in 2004.

Park Place Plaza, 2501 Texas Avenue S, College Station

View from 1999

Courtesy of Kovak & Co. Real Estate

Winn-Dixie Marketplace

Courtesy of The Eagle

Courtesy of YKYFBCS

Courtesy of The Battalion

Courtesy of Project HOLD

Kentucky Fried Chicken opened in 1986 and remodeled around 2007.

Winn-Dixie Marketplace opened in 1985 and eventually closed in 1995 due to the competition of other grocery stores. The space then became Lack's Furniture in 1997 and eventually closed in 2010. It is now the site of Ace Hardware and Planet Fitness.

Courtesy of The Eagle

Chapter 22: Southwest Parkway, College Station

Arby's,
1800 Southwest Pkwy

Courtesy of The Eagle

Opened in 1983 and remodeled in 2003.

Courtesy of The Courier

Shipley Do-Nuts,
1716 Southwest Pkwy

Opened in 1985

7-Eleven,
1712 Southwest Pkwy

Courtesy of Google Earth

Opened in 1985 and became an E-Z Mart in 1993. E-Z Mart then closed around 2008, and the building was remodeled for Fuzzy's Tacos in 2009.

CarePlus Medical Center,
1712 Southwest Pkwy

Courtesy of The Eagle

Opened in 1985 and moved to 2411 Texas Avenue, S College Station in 1992.

Plaza 3 Theater, 226 Southwest Pkwy, College Station

Courtesy of The Eagle

Courtesy of Project HOLD

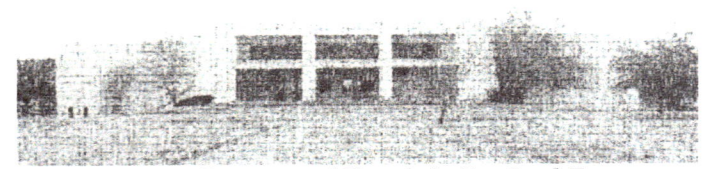

Courtesy of Kovak & Co. Real Estate

Owned by the Schulman family, the Plaza 3 opened in 1985 as a three-screen theater and closed shortly after in 1990. The physical structure of the building was not up to code and is what led to its sudden closure. The space was used for other businesses throughout the years and is now the site of Brazos Fellowship Church.

Chapter 23: Texas Avenue South to Highway 6, College Station

Kettle Restaurant, 2502 Texas Avenue, College Station

Courtesy of Google Earth

Courtesy of Carnegie History Center

Opened in 1983 and closed in 2022. The building was then demolished for Salad and Go in 2023.

Pelican's Wharf, 2500 Texas Avenue, College Station

Courtesy of The Eagle   *Courtesy of The Battalion*

Opened in 1977 and became popular restaurant known for its seafood and steaks. Pelican's Wharf eventually closed in 1995 and the space became Pasghetti's Restaurant the same year and then Royer's Café in 1997. Royer's closed shortly after in 1999 and the site became Nail Spa in 2005, which is still open today.

199

Fort Shiloh Steakhouse, 2528 Texas Avenue S, College Station

Courtesy of The Eagle

Courtesy of Project HOLD

Courtesy of The Eagle

Ken Martin's Fort Shiloh Steakhouse opened in 1977 and became a staple restaurant in the area. The building was designed as an Indian fort, and inside were different themed rooms of western culture. The waiters and waitresses also wore western clothing, and the menu consisted of steak, chicken, fajitas, and salad. After many years, Fort Shiloh closed around 1995 and the building sat vacant for several years. In 2005, the building was eventually demolished and is now the site of an empty lot.

South College Station, 1986

Courtesy of Insite Magazine

College Station Police Department, 2611 Texas Avenue S

Courtesy of The Eagle

Opened in 1978, moving from 1207 Texas Avenue. In 2020, a new police department was built at 800 Krenek Tap Rd and the space is now IL Texas Aggieland High School.

Kmart, 2700 Texas Avenue S, College Station

Courtesy of Project HOLD

Opened in 1974 as the area's only Kmart and eventually closed in 1994.

Piggly Wiggly, 2700 Texas Avenue S, College Station

Courtesy of The Eagle

Opened in 1977 next to Kmart and closed in 1985.

Putt Putt Golf, 1705 Valley View Dr, College Station

Courtesy of 1989 A&M Consolidated High School Yearbook

Opened in 1987 and closed around 2006.

Ira's, 2702 Texas Avenue, College Station

Courtesy of Insite Magazine

Opened in 1983 as a store that sold liquor, chocolates, and featured a bakery inside. Ira's closed in 1985 and the space became Ferreri's Italian Restaurant from 1991 to around 1996. Taste of China Restaurant then opened in the location in 2000 and eventually closed in 2015. The space has since been Q Beauty (opened in 2016).

Walmart, 1815 Brothers Blvd, College Station

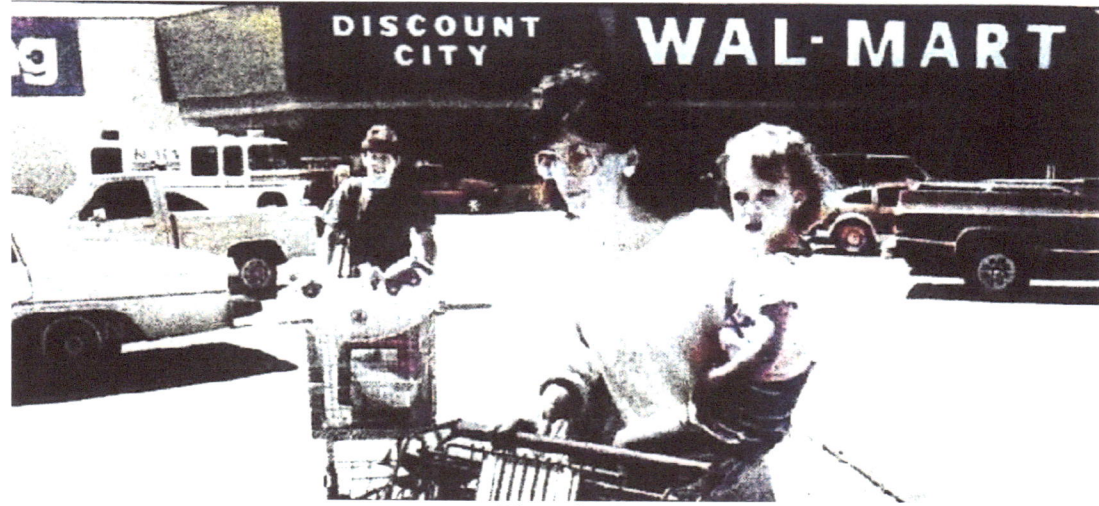

Sign seen from Texas Avenue

Photo by Dave McDermand from The Eagle

Courtesy of the family of Jimmy Jackson

Opened in 1988 and remodeled in 1995 and again in 2010.

Jimmy Jackson Exxon Station, 2801 Texas Avenue S, College Station

Courtesy of the family of Jimmy Jackson

Opened around 1984 and became Franky's Exxon in 2002, which is still open today.

Diamond Shamrock Gas Station, 3129 Texas Avenue S, College Station

Image Capture 9/12/2006, Courtesy of Google Earth

Opened in 1987 as a Tenneco Station and became a Diamond Shamrock in 1989. The gas station was then demolished for a Burger King in 2007.

& Trust
101 North Texas Avenue

MANOR EAST
2700 Texas Avenue

culpepper plaza
1500 Texas Avenue South

Courtesy of The Eagle

Contributions were made by: The Battalion, Cushing Memorial Library, Carnegie History Center, The Eagle (Through Licensed Agreement), Texas A&M University Yearbooks, Bryan High School Yearbooks, A&M Consolidated High School Yearbooks, Kemp High School Yearbooks, Up from cotton: a pictorial history book of blacks in the Brazos Valley, Insite Magazine, The Courier, The Texas Aggie Magazine, Project HOLD, Brazos Heritage Society, 150.bryantx.gov, Texashistory.unt.edu, Flickr, Google Earth, Maps.bryantx.gov, Historicaerials.com, Csroadsandretail.blogspot.com, Kovak & Co. Real Estate, Osborn & Vane Architects, Inc, Emporis.com, City of Bryan YouTube, City of College Station YouTube, Loopnet.com, Blinn College, Archive.org, Bryan-College Station Visitors' Guide, Brazos Valley Area-Wide Phone Book, Jose's Restaurant, Texags.com, Save the Signs Facebook, Copy Corner Facebook, College Station Pawn Facebook, Former Texas Division Associates Facebook, and the Facebook group: You Know You're From Bryan/College Station When.....

Any photographs not cited were taken by me or are from my own family photo albums.

Some photographs were altered to provide color or enhance details.

About the Author

Michael Gomez was born and raised in Bryan, Texas and attended Bryan and College Station schools. He earned his Bachelor's degree in Urban & Regional Planning at Texas A&M University (Class of 2024). In his free time, he loves to draw, listen to and collect music, and study history.

For more information or other inquiries, please email: mgj2332@gmail.com

Printed in the USA
CPSIA information can be obtained
at www.ICGtesting.com
LVHW050336090524
779692LV00004B/73